CW00435240

CREATIVE
VEGETARIAN
COOKERY

CREATIVE VEGETARIAN COOKERY

CLARE FERGUSON

EBURY PRESS LONDON

Published by Ebury Press
Division of The National Magazine
Company Limited
Colquhoun House
27-37 Broadwick Street
London W1V 1FR

First Impression 1986

Text Copyright © 1986 by Clare Ferguson
Photographs Copyright © 1986 by The
National Magazine Company Limited
Illustrations Copyright © 1986 by Toula Antonakos

All rights reserved. No part of this publication may be
reproduced, stored in a retrieval system or
transmitted in any form or by any means, electronic,
mechanical, photocopying, recording, or otherwise,
without the prior permission of the copyright owner.

ISBN 0 85223 532 1 (hardback)
     0 85223 592 5 (paperback)

Edited by Yvonne McFarlane
Art Directed by Frank Phillips
Designed by Grub Street Design, London
Photographs by Bryce Attwell
Illustrations by Toula Antonakos
Food prepared for photography by Clare Ferguson
Styling by Cathy Sinker
Props (linen, glass, china, antiques) for the
photographs provided by:
Nina Fuller, Ayres and Graces, Eastgates Antiques,
Fritzies, Alfie's Market, 13–25 Church Street,
London NW8

Filmset in Great Britain by
Advanced Filmsetters (Glasgow) Ltd

Printed in Great Britain at
The University Press,
Cambridge

CONTENTS

A Cook's Confessions
(7)

Absolute Beginnings
(8)

Bold Beginnings
(10)

Soup Making and Stock Taking
(40)

The Central Course
(61)

Visible Extras
(115)

Cured, Pickled and Preserved Garnishes
(131)

Happy Endings
(139)

Index
(158)

For
my family and many friends
who inspired me
to develop and share
the ideas in this book
and those colleagues
who have helped produce
these words and images.

A Cook's Confessions

VITALITY AND a lively style of eating and drinking come naturally to those who enjoy life and who have been fortunate enough to have found food exciting and rewarding since childhood.

But much depends upon keeping an open mind. Just as we now know that our adult physique is predetermined to some extent by patterns set in infancy (and a cell structure established very early in development), the positive and negative factors in sociability and eating start early too.

Good food is a potent force: for bargaining, for exercising power, for pleasure, for learning, as well as being necessary for good health. Food can represent fun and be used to express personality and identity.

How a person eats can certainly convey ideas. I firmly believe I can tell a lot about a person by the kind of food and drinks they might choose in a restaurant. I am always curious to see the reaction I get to certain food-orientated questions or the expression upon people's faces if I suggest certain drinks, certain dishes. Some see my curiosity as a challenge, others a duty, one or two a threat, and others may not even deem it worthy of a serious reply or reaction. As a cook and a writer about food it is one aspect of my profession to notice how people react to food and drink—what they buy (or what they influence others into buying for them), what they ignore, look down on, listen to, and laugh about, and what causes them confusion. Most of all I care about what incites their curiosity, fascination and pleasure. There is much to know, so many ways to acquire that knowledge yet so little redress (once one has a hungry group of family or friends, seated, expectant around the table) if it all goes wrong, or nobody likes what you have produced.

What pleases me, and, I think, many people who care about cooking, is that providing good meals (for oneself and for others) as well as promoting a feeling of healthy well-being, and interest in what is good and is new, is a constant source of satisfaction and delight.

We must eat in order to live. Creating appetite and maintaining enthusiasm for food instead of merely shovelling in fuel seems an idea eminently worth working towards and trying for.

Creative Vegetarian Cookery is for likeminded people of all ages and tastes who have one thing in common: they like cooking and enjoy eating good food and the journey of exploration this entails.

ABSOLUTEBEGINNINGS

'An understanding of what food is and how cooking works does no violence to the art of cuisine, destroys no delightful mystery. Instead, the mystery expands from matters of expertise and taste to encompass the hidden patterns and wonderful coincidences of nature.'

'On Food and Cooking' Harold McGee

GOOD COOKERY is an art which should hold no fears for anyone. Most people who enjoy food are always happy to learn more about it, for understanding makes for greater pleasure. Good eating, the natural outcome of good cooking, should be appreciated for what it is, a garden of evergreen delights, where knowledge, abandon and restraint each play their part.

Writing a decent cookery book of original recipe ideas involves observation, research, imagination and persuasion on the part of the author. Selecting it, is an act of curiosity and good faith on the part of the reader. I write for today: for people who have already begun to develop an instinct for the proper selection of ingredients, for the best techniques for preparing and cooking foods, and for those who wish to learn how to serve them with a flourish, with individual style. Though discerning, these individuals also have come to recognize that good food and drink always remains a voyage of discovery. These same people also know that good dining involves judgment, and that eating sensibly and well is not a duty, it is one of life's good things.

In my case, avid travelling, the kitchens of friends, wide reading of old texts as well as up-to-the-minute reports, the traditions of my childhood, specialist food research and good restaurants, have all helped to shape my eclectic culinary views. I learn, borrow and adapt shamelessly from near and far. *Creative Vegetarian Cookery* is written for enthusiastic omnivores: those keen to try a wide range of foods. This book does not constitute an absolute vegetarian regime; only part will be useful for vegans or fruitarians. It is merely a collection of my own recipes, menu suggestions and ideas which are vegetarian in content.

In my view, one of the best ways of preparing meals is to search out the finest, freshest possible raw materials I can afford, do as little as possible (using all the technical expertise I have gained) to make them taste and look good, use as much wit and imagination as I can summon to present them beautifully, then sit back with anticipation, and savour the results amongst amiable table companions whose reactions will be of interest to me, and whose pleasure I cherish. That I may have learned new combinations, preferences and often, almost by accident, new techniques along the way, is part of the charm of cooking. If you cook at all, then learning is unavoidable for food presents us with a series of curious and absorbing questions—What is that funny vegetable? What do you do with this peculiar fruit?

Finding out by trial and experiment, by reading, asking and observing others is what good cooking hinges upon. Learning the (culinary) rules is one thing. Knowing how and when to break them is quite another.

Today's cookery books should, ideally, reflect the desire, on the part of the cooking and eating public, to know more about the food we put into our mouths. A general awareness of what is going on in the pan, plus a little imagination, will compensate for unfamiliar ingredients, or techniques, or lack of experience.

This book of recipes which I have devised during these last months is only a beginning. The vegetarian kitchen has no end to its possibilities. The raw materials are vast, the range so great. To me, a passionate omnivore, this book has provided the chance to view, with a different eye, the possibilities that the plant world offers for the making of delectable dishes. For, in the past, vegetables have often played a supporting role. But once we establish them firmly as an honourable core at the centre of the menu, they can suddenly assume a glorious new significance.

Many people have become aware of the need for more fruit and vegetables—both raw and cooked—in their diet. They want, as do I, variety. They do not, however, wish either to spend too long slaving away in the kitchen, nor to produce unpalatable dishes. My emphasis, therefore, has been on wise choice, delicious and nutritious combinations, streamlined techniques and creative presentation. To help readers plan their menus, I frequently include wines, digestifs, cocktails and other drinks which may precede or accompany or follow each dish. What has become specially important to me, however, is my own judicious addition of one or several specially relevant 'taste-accents' given by some sympathetic ingredient: a particular herb or salad leaf, an aromatic oil, a fruit vinegar, a toasted seed, nut or spice garnish. This creative detail in my view can make or break the dish, and make it memorable or not. Also important are my unusual or unique ways of handling, arranging or combining foods to better show off their special charms.

Creative eating

For most creative eaters the joys of the table extend beyond mere cookery skills and technique: each food should evoke pleasure, for the eye and the palate. Successful dishes may bring with them memories of times, places, people, ideas and happenings.

Because it can be both stressful and impractical to attempt more than one unfamiliar recipe at any one meal, I have often suggested simple, stylish but time-honoured accompaniments, such as a particular cheese, a wine I have enjoyed, a certain type of bread, crisp salad leaves or seasonal fresh fruits as 'supports'. Remember the appeal of simple things, especially seasonal ingredients.

In planning meals, formality matters less than an innate balance. Meals may be relatively structured, totally unstructured, arranged in a traditional ethnic way, adventurous or capricious. But proper variety in tastes and textures within each meal, lightness and richness, colour and consistency, with no one ingredient (or group of ingredients) occurring too frequently throughout, will mean that it is likely that you have constructed a sound meal. Empty plates and smiling faces are the best indications of success. Though food alone surely cannot cure all ills, it certainly has a major part to play in our well-being.

9

Bold Beginnings

HIS, THE first chapter in the book, contains bold beginnings of several kinds. Here you will find refreshing drinks, nourishing breakfasts, appetizers, snacks, healthful breads and robust seasonings (alternatives to salt and pepper). Within the breakfasts, brunches, snack-type foods, lunches and meal-beginning appetizers included in this initial chapter, are embodied a new approach. It happens, almost by accident, to be vegetarian also. Its emphasis is upon the best, lightest, most superb elements of freshness. It is part of the bright and the actively taste-positive. Fresh juices which retain their goodness, colour, taste and scent make delectable starts to the day. The most brilliant beginning, the boldest step you can take into a new morning, is by making one of my 'liquid refreshers'—fresh fruit and vegetable juice mixtures. I have a passionate (and probably unreasonable) dislike of fruit juice in cans or cartons. In the course of researching, testing and writing the recipes in this book, I bought an electric juicer with which I developed the 'liquid refreshers' section. Hence, some of the fresh fruit, fruit-and-vegetable or fruit-and-wine cocktails are only truly possible if you own a fruit and vegetable juicer (as distinct from a citrus juicer)—mine can wring juice from celery and spinach as well as carrots, onions, apples and oranges, in the twinkling of an eye, with extraordinarily delicious results.

I feel that people who really care about taste and flavour may well feel that this device is worth investing in (it costs roughly the equivalent of a respectable 3-course lunch, with wine, for two in a restaurant). An electric juicer will reduce many nutrient- and juice-high foods to a concentrated liquid 'essence', full of goodness, in seconds. The volume, colour, intensity and scent of the juice is quite different to that achieved by using a blender and, say, iced water. But wherever there is an alternative method of producing the recipe I have given it. Sometimes there is no comparison whatsoever, so I have suggested that the recipe not be attempted.

Some of my Bold Beginning drinks are definitely not for everyday: they include delicious but expensive fruits. On the other hand, if a breakfast beverage is sustaining and prevents you from being tempted by unhealthy, high-cost, high-calorie snacks during the course of the morning, then it has surely fulfilled its purpose. Once again, it is all a matter of balance.

Many of the recipes in this chapter, whether based on eggs, cheese or nuts, have been designed as bold and brave frameworks for your own style of eating, there are even one or two curious yeast bread recipes made using a new dried yeast which can raise dough with the ease of baking-powder. Read the list of ingredients carefully. Dry yeast is not at all the same as dry micronized (easybake or easyblend) yeast, which is the type I advocate, for simplicity's sake. You can, if you like, make, slice, wrap and freeze these loaves for immediate thawing and warming (or toasting) at an instant's notice. New ways to cut, shape, spread, toast and present breads (such as the recipe for grignons and the lentil-filled 'tartines' in this chapter) along with Japanese-style rice dainties, and tiny pickled quails' eggs—all are intended to give bright ideas as a basis for your own personalized cuisine.

I *have* included two specific breakfast recipes. One is a recipe for delicious, homemade porridge (not the instant, rolled oats kind but the *real* kind, used by the Scots for centuries) with an untraditional manner of presentation, the other a recipe for 'snack-muesli' (make up the recipe at the weekend and it will last a healthily hungry family of considerable size all the way through the week). It is also a far better 'nibble' or snack food than bought potato crisps, for example, and far more cost and energy effective, too.

ALTERNATIVE SEASONINGS

To prevent the readers of this book from having too heavy a dependence upon the valuable, but sometimes over-used salt and pepper, I have devised for this chapter some 'creative seasonings'. All very low in salt (for the health conscious) they are aromatic and flavoursome—often underpinned by seaweed (a real newcomer to westerners, but not to the Japanese), spices, herbs, seeds and nuts, treated and combined in various ways. There is also a hot seasoning, for replacing traditional pepper on your table. Make them up and keep them in pretty pots or jars in the fridge and use them as your bold beginning to a new chapter of lighter cuisine.

BOLD BEGINNINGS TO A NEW EATING STYLE

Just as there is a resurgence of interest in real food, real breakfasts, 'new classicism', there is also a general move towards less 'structured' eating patterns amongst those who have the confidence to re-think their food and their needs. These trends, of course, I heartily applaud. Neither are anything other than lively, useful and positively good. The eating of a good and sensible diet is no strict regime; no prison: it is a celebration of some of the natural world's fascinating, edible things.

The recipes in this chapter, then, can be fitted in at any time of day or night. They are the platform for a new approach to food and a new style of eating as exemplified in the rest of this book. Accept these recipes for what they are: often radical, frequently inspirational, but never dull. And because of their adaptability they can take one right through the spectrum from Monday to Sunday, from dawn to dusk, from February to September, with a special liveliness.

11

LIQUID REFRESHERS

MIDSUMMER FROTH
(Illustrated facing page 64)

GOOD THINGS often cost one dear and this cocktail (with or without champagne of the top quality) is not exactly one to drink every day. Keep as many celebrations on hand, however, as you can manage: it is a stunning recipe: fresh, clean and utterly appetizing in taste. The colour is a brilliant scarlet. What a reason to remember midsummer! The impact of the scarlet froth lasts for some time. Although a juicer is the only appliance to achieve the required concentration of colour, taste and clarity, a blender version can be attempted but the colour and vividness of taste are far less effective, though pleasant.

MAKES 600 ml (1 pint)
SERVES 2, 4 OR 6

2 bananas, (peeled weight about 175 g (6 oz)), quartered
350 g (12 oz) punnet of fresh strawberries, hulled
1 lemon peeled and cubed, (zest shredded and reserved)

1 orange peeled and cubed, (zest shredded and reserved)
2–4 ice cubes
600 ml (1 pint) dry champagne, chilled (or sparkling Saumur or sparkling mineral water) optional

Into a juicer, process in successive batches some of each of the bananas, strawberries, lemon and orange cubes with some ice cubes, to yield a blended juice.

(If using a blender add the first 2 fruits, the juice of the citrus fruits, in batches, half at a time with 150 ml ($\frac{1}{4}$ pint) of liquid of choice and blend until smooth. Repeat this process with the second batch.)

Pour into 2 large goblets (or giant mugs if being taken without added alcohol) or pour some into 4 or 6 large champagne flutes. Top up with the sparkling liquid of your choice. (This makes enough for 2 glasses for each guest.)

The blender version is salmon-pink, not scarlet, and makes 1 litre (1$\frac{3}{4}$ pints) of milder tasting beverage—use large glasses.

LASSITUDE COCKTAIL

(Illustrated facing page 64)

N OT FAR removed from Lassi, that spicy, iced yogurt drink so often served with Indian meals, this rather original version contains fresh orange juice within its pastel coolness.

Served as a long drink it is soothing, gentle and remarkably calming: its name is both descriptive and a word game. As a short drink it would make a delightful start to a sophisticated meal. The cocktail may be made in a blender although a juicer gives more refined tastes and textures. The yield is the same. Follow the preparations in parentheses for the blender version, which will be more grainy, but still acceptable.

MAKES 600 ml (1 pint)
SERVES 2 OR 4

---

225 g (8 oz) or half a cucumber, skin
  removed, finely cubed
1 large handful of fresh mint (finely
  shredded)
1 orange peeled and cubed, (zest shredded
  and reserved)
4–8 ice cubes

125 g (4 oz) fromage blanc battu
60 ml (4 tbsp) mineral water
few shakes of salt

TO SERVE:
additional mint sprigs
reserved orange zest
additional mineral water (optional)

Into a juicer, process in successive batches some of each of the cucumber, mint, orange flesh and 1 or 2 ice cubes to yield a blended juice. Add the Fromage Blanc and whisk until smooth and blended.

(If using a blender add the first 5 ingredients to the blender (with 1 or 2 ice cubes and a little iced mineral water) and blend until smooth. Add remaining ice cubes, blend again.)

Season the mixture to taste, stirring well. Pour into 2 large glasses or 4 smaller goblets.

Top up with a little mineral water, as required. Scatter over the reserved zest and add mint sprigs to garnish.

*F*ingers of nutty brown rye bread taste good with this. The
blender version is more a meal prelude than the drink to start the day.

RUSSIAN PINK COCKTAIL

THIS PRETTY concoction is vividly pink and looks ravishing when the orange shreds are added as part of the final flourish. It has great charm, tremendously clean tastes, and would make a good large morning, lunch or smaller pre-meal drink. Because of its rich ingredients it can be a meal in itself though the effect is not, in the end, anything other than sustaining. This cocktail can be made equally well in a juicer or in a blender—the results are similar and the yield the same. Follow the preparations in parentheses for the blender version, which is a trifle more grainy.

MAKES 600 ml (1 pint)
SERVES 2 OR 4

225 g (8 oz), or ½, cucumber, skin removed, cubed (or grated)
100 g (4 oz) or 1 or 2, raw young beets, cubed (or grated)
small handful of beetroot tops (or red lettuce, feuilles de chêne) (shredded)
150 ml (¼ pint) soured cream or buttermilk
1 orange peeled and cubed (shredded zest reserved)

4–8 ice cubes
a little mineral water
few shakes of salt
freshly ground black pepper

TO SERVE:
reserved orange zest
additional beet tops or red lettuce, shredded (optional)

Into a juicer, process in successive batches some of each of the cucumber, the beets, the leaves, orange flesh and 1 or 2 ice cubes to yield a blended juice. Add the soured cream and whisk or shake with the remaining ice cubes until smooth and blended.

(If using a blender add the first 5 ingredients to the blender, with 1 or 2 ice cubes and a little iced mineral water, and blend until smooth. Add remaining ice cubes. Blend again.)

Season to taste with salt and pepper, stirring well. Pour into 2 large glasses or 4 smaller tumblers.

Scatter over the reserved zest and a few shreds of beet tops or red lettuce.

BOLIVAR SOPHISTICATE

SIMPLE FRUITY tastes are sharpened into attention by the addition of one or two unexpected extras: angostura bitters (originally a distillate of herbs and spices dreamed up as a tonic for the Venezuelan army in 1824) and fruit-flavoured vinegar. The sandy golden colour is, too, rather apt and it is guaranteed to arouse interest in a thirsty and hungry throat. The crushed ice should be used merely to chill the glasses. Drink this undiluted, for a large 'meal-in-one' breakfast or brunch or as an appetizer before a main meal. This beverage can only be attempted using a juicer—no other appliance can achieve the desired effect.

MAKES 400–600 ml ($\frac{3}{4}$–1 pint)

SERVES 2–4

2 large bananas, peeled and quartered
2 medium carrots, scrubbed and chopped
1 orange, peeled, flesh quartered
1 lime, peeled, flesh quartered
2 tomatoes, quartered

150 ml ($\frac{1}{4}$ pint) chilled, natural yogurt
5 ml (1 tsp) angostura bitters
15 ml (1 tbsp) raspberry vinegar (or other
 fruit-flavoured vinegar)
crushed ice

Into a juicer, process in successive batches some of each of the bananas, carrots, orange, lime and tomatoes to yield a blended juice. Whisk in the yogurt, bitters and vinegar and chill until very cold.

Fill 2 large or 4 medium-sized glasses with crushed ice. Just before serving, discard the ice, fill the glasses and drink the 'tonic' freshly cold.

SESAME EGG FROTH

(Illustrated facing page 64)

A NUTRITIOUS AND sustaining yet delightful beverage which looks very decorative with its cloud of sweet frothy 'meringue' on top and speckled seeds. Tahini, a toasted sesame seed purée or 'cream' (which is bought in jars), tastes rather like a subtle version of peanut butter. Full of flavour and goodness and quite enriching, is an important part of this recipe. Because tahini is so concentrated, it is necessary to blend it with some boiling (not merely hot) water just before it joins the remaining ingredients.

MAKES 300 ml ($\frac{1}{2}$ pint)

SERVES 2

45 ml (3 level tbsp) tahini
75 ml (5 tbsp) boiling water
4 oranges, freshly squeezed (finely shredded
 zest reserved)
1 lime, freshly squeezed
5 ml (1 tsp) citrus flower water
1 egg yolk

TOPPING FROTH:
5 ml (1 level tsp) Hymettus honey
1 egg white
pinch salt
10 ml (2 tsp) sesame seeds, pan-toasted
crushed ice or ice cubes

Stir the tahini and the boiling water together to make a light creamy mixture.

Blend or shake the fruit juices, the citrus flower water and yolk together until frothy. Add the tahini 'cream' and blend again.

In a separate small bowl, whisk the honey, egg white and salt to a light, pale, frothy mixture. Pour the sesame juice mixture into 2 chilled glasses (each containing some crushed ice or ice cubes). Top each with half of the froth, and sprinkle with the seeds.

Eve's Tamanrasset

THE COMBINED flavours of peanut, chilli and of fruit somehow suggest African images to me—sand, salt lakes and heat. Here is a nut enriched meal-in-one which has a wide variety of possibilities for brunch, lunch or supper. Harissa paste (a hot condiment which includes chilli, caraway, cumin and coriander) is often found in delicatessens, ethnic markets and specialty stores. Although I prefer to use harissa, other seasonings such as Indonesian sambal oelek, or even a little lime pickle (both proprietary products, readily available) could be substituted.

This recipe could really be described as a sort of liquid spiced fruit 'curry', or cold soup, as well as being a sustaining drink. It is best made using a blender which yields a creamy result—like a super milk shake. You can eat this (very chilled) with a teaspoon, or drink it from the glass. Try it on teenagers and the very young.

MAKES 600 ml (1 pint)
SERVES 2, 4 OR 6

45 ml (3 level tbsp) smooth peanut butter
60 ml (4 tbsp) boiling water
2.5–5 ml ($\frac{1}{2}$–1 level tsp) harissa paste (or sambal oelek or lime pickle)
60 ml (4 tbsp) low fat natural yogurt
1 lime, freshly squeezed (zest freshly shredded and reserved)

1 lemon, freshly squeezed (zest freshly shredded and reserved)
1 large mango, skinned, seeded and cubed
1 banana, peeled, cubed

TO SERVE:
reserved zests (optional)

Combine the first 3 ingredients and blend until smooth. Add yogurt, process again.

Add the lime and lemon juices and the mango and banana flesh to the blender and blend to a creamy texture.

Pour into 2, 4 or 6 chilled goblets. Decorate with the reserved zests, if wished.

STATISTICAL REVIVER

IT IS said there are 3 kinds of untruth: lies, damned lies and statistics. Quails' eggs often fall into the last category: admired often and by many people, few but professional cooks dare to use them in their cookery! Few will ever admit to this, however. There is a simplicity, even ingenuousness in the flavours of this drink, and it takes some seconds for the palate to distinguish them all. Serve it for breakfast (without the alcohol) or as a pre-lunch or supper drink with the alcohol left in. This delicious drink can only be made using a juicer—no other appliance gives the equivalent result. I think the fruit brandy is integral to this drink.

MAKES 600 ml (1 pint)
SERVES 2 OR 4

---

225 g (8 oz), or 2 or 3, carrots, scrubbed
 and chopped
1 orange, flesh only, peeled and quartered
275 g (10 oz) or 2 large, apples (Cox's
 Orange), quartered
8–10 ice cubes
60 ml (4 tbsp) single cream

60 ml (4 tbsp) fruit eau de vie, such as
 Calvados (optional)
3 quails' eggs (or 1 hen's egg)

TO SERVE:
1.25 ml ($\frac{1}{4}$ tsp) ground cinnamon

Into a juicer, process in successive batches some of each of the carrot, the orange and apple chunks with 1 or 2 ice cubes, to give a blended juice.

Whisk in the remaining ice cubes, cream and, if wished, the eau de vie and quails' eggs until smooth and frothy.

Pour into 2 large balloon glasses or 4 smaller goblets. Sprinkle some cinnamon on top of each of the individual glasses.

17

MELISANTO ZOE

THE NAME I have given to this invention as well as being a reference to sweetness, is a reference to health and life. The drink contains distinguished ingredients, all of them tenderly scented. Drink this concoction while it is still fresh and frothy at its deep crimson best. The faint heat it causes at the back of the throat is surprisingly pleasant and stops the sweetness from becoming cloying. Top up the drink, if liked, with some good blanc de blancs (if you feel expansive) and enjoy an altogether splendid sense of well-being. A good drink for first thing in the morning (without the wine) or for lunch or early evening, when the addition of wine is eminently suitable.

MAKES 600 ml (1 pint)
SERVES 2 OR 4

550 g (1¼ lb) scented ogen melon, skinned, seeded and cubed
175 g (6 oz) punnet of fresh raspberries
1 large, (about 225 g/8 oz), fresh pear peeled, quartered

30 ml (1 level tbsp) orange blossom honey
1.25 ml (¼ tsp) cayenne pepper
150 ml (¼ pint) dry, crisp, white wine (blanc de blancs), or mineral water, chilled

Into a juicer, process in successive batches the first 3 fruits to yield a blended juice.

(Alternatively, purée them using a blender, adding enough of the chilled wine or mineral water to keep the mixture moving.)

To the juices add the honey, cayenne and the appropriate amount of chilled wine or mineral water and whisk (or blend) briefly.

Pour the drink into 2 chilled large goblets or tumblers, or 4 smaller glasses, with, (if wished), a few additional ice cubes, or some crushed ice at the base of each glass.

If using a juicer, smaller volume and a super-concentrated 'essence' is obtained. A blender will give reasonable (but not the same) results. Follow preparation in parentheses for the blended version which makes 1 litre (1¾ pints) and is a deeper, opaque bronze colour.

BLACKROSE COCKTAIL

CITRUS FLAVOUR with undertones of peach, musky rose and deep red berries: what a lively combination! This fresh fruit drink is delicious, decorative and healthful. Drink it for breakfast, (without the alcohol), for brunch or very chilled before a dinner or supper meal, with the eau de vie added. Made in quantity, served in large jugs with extra mineral water to hand, it would be stylish and interesting for a late summer supper party, perhaps. One can taste the goodness—even if frozen and barely-thawed berries are used out of necessity. Do not attempt this elegant beverage without a juicer: other appliances cannot achieve the same result.

MAKES 450–600 ml ($\frac{3}{4}$–1 pint)

SERVES 2–4

125 g (4 oz) fresh (or frozen) blackberries
2 clementines or satsumas, peeled
1 pink-fleshed or yellow grapefruit, peeled, cut into eighths
2 ripe peaches, stoned, quartered

1 lemon, peeled, quartered
1.25–2.5 ml ($\frac{1}{4}$–$\frac{1}{2}$ tsp) rose water
50–150 ml (2–5 fl oz) chilled sparkling mineral water
30 ml (2 tbsp) fruit eau de vie (Poire William, Quetch, Mirabelle etc)

Into a juicer, process in successive batches some of each of the blackberries, clementines, grapefruit, peaches and lemon, to yield a blended juice. Add the rose water, mineral water to taste and the eau de vie if wished.

Pour into ice-cold glasses, (perhaps previously frosted around the rim with lemon and caster sugar) with some crushed ice at the base of each drink, if liked.

TORTOLA SUNSHINE

WHAT MORE wonderful pleasure than to roll out of bed to the sparkle of a fruit potion so achingly sharp, sweet and fresh that it defies description! One can easily summon up tropical islands, fresh air and sunshine with a cool glass of this in one's hand. This golden drink is a superlative beginning to any day, any project, any undertaking. However it can only be made using a juicer—no other appliance gives the equivalent concentrated clear, strong result.

MAKES 600 ml (1 pint)

SERVES 2, 4 OR 6

1 large, (about 1.1 kg (2$\frac{1}{2}$ lb) before preparing) fresh pineapple, skinned, chopped into 2.5 cm (1 inch) chunks
2 ripe fresh peaches, stoned, and segmented

8–12 ice cubes
150 ml ($\frac{1}{4}$ pint) sparkling or still dry white wine (or soda) optional
4 small edible flowers or aromatic leaves

Into a juicer, process in successive batches some of each of the pineapple, peaches and half the ice cubes.

Pour into chilled glass mugs, goblets, or small tumblers. Top up, if wished, with the ice, and add wine to give a more ethereal effect, (though it must be said that the pure fruit version has great charm on its own). Add a flower or leaf decoration (e.g. pot marigolds or violets).

Avant-Goûts

Lentilles Tiedes, Tartines Tapenaro

(Warm lentils with olive-spread bread)

IN THIS recipe, olive-green lentils are cooked until tender (they do not need prior soaking), then spooned on to small pieces of French bread which have been spread with olive, lemon and mushroom purée. It's hardly a classical *tapénade* (which must contain capers, from the word 'tapena', the origin of the name, and, correctly, tuna and anchovy, as well as lemon) but something approximating it.

This version contains raw mushrooms, a touch of oil and a lot of pepper. It is delicious, and very rich, like a sort of non-marine fish roe. It looks grape-dark or black, depending upon the origin of the olives you have selected. The sweet mildness of the lentils is interesting in such strong-tasting company. This recipe makes more of the olive spread than is needed for the tartines so keep it in a sealed pot in the refrigerator and use it for other occasions—it keeps well. It is good served with crisp celery sticks.

——— SERVES 4 ———

LENTILS:
225 g (8 oz) green lentils (small Le Puy lentils or the larger slate-green type), rinsed
1 litre (1¾ pints) cold water
1 fresh bouquet garni (fresh bay, parsley and thyme)
8–12 green peppercorns
1 medium carrot, quartered
1 small onion, peeled and quartered

TAPENARO:
24 black olives, stoned (Provençal, Greek or Italian)

50 g (2 oz) button mushrooms, chopped
10 ml (2 tsp) fruity olive oil (Provençal, Greek or Italian)
15 ml (1 tbsp) freshly squeezed lemon juice
freshly ground black pepper

DRESSING:
45 ml (3 tbsp) fruity olive oil (Provençal, Greek or Italian)
45 ml (3 tbsp) white wine vinegar
1 garlic clove, skinned and chopped
2 spring onions, finely sliced
1 French bread stick
celery sticks, with leaves

Put rinsed lentils, water, herbs, peppercorns, carrot and onion into a flameproof saucepan (preferably enamelled or ceramic). Bring to the boil, cover, reduce heat and simmer for 25 minutes or until the vegetables are bite-tender. Drain (reserving liquid and vegetables for soup). Preheat the grill.

To make the *tapénaro* paste, put the olives, mushrooms, oil and lemon into the blender or food processor and blend or process to a thick dark purée. (To increase volume and mildness, add some of the chopped cooked carrot from cooking the lentils.) Make the (fairly sharp) dressing for the lentils by shaking or stirring the oil, vinegar, garlic and spring onions together. Toss the lentils well in this dressing.

Cut the French bread in half lengthways, then into quarters crossways. Use a teaspoon to hollow them out a little. (Crumbs can be used in another recipe.) Spread the hollowed out pieces of bread lightly with the *tapénaro*.

Grill the bread until the edges begin to darken and become crusty. Spoon a quarter of the lentils in their dressing over each serving. Leave whole or cut into smaller pieces, if wished. Serve while still warm, with celery sticks.

A rough and lusty Provençal rosé, or a red wine from the Toulon area (such as Bandol) would be good with this dish. Alternatively, try a really dry Cassis (dry white) from the seaside village of that name. If this is a first course, this dish could be followed by rice-thickened purée soup and then perhaps a red-leafed salad with cheese croûtons and, perhaps, a blackcurrant ice or sorbet.

Plantain Appetizers With Poppy Seeds

BLACK-SKINNED plantains, which must only be eaten cooked, not raw, have a curious dry fleshiness. A slight tannin content gives them bitterness which can be interesting when combined with other nutty tastes. In this recipe the plantain slices are simply oven-dried with poppy seed to enliven them. Use them in place of nuts or crisps beforehand, or during a meal as an accompaniment, particularly with Caribbean, Malaysian, Indonesian and African style dishes. When sufficiently cooked the texture becomes quite leathery to the touch.

——— SERVES 4 ———

2–3 medium-sized, black-skinned plantains
30 ml (2 level tbsp) blue poppy seeds

15 ml (1 level tbsp) Polyglot Seasoning, see page 38, (optional)

Leave the skin on the plantains and slice them crossways into 6 mm ($\frac{1}{4}$ inch) slices. Spread them on 2 sheets of greaseproof paper which have been lightly covered with seeds (and seasoning, if used). Sprinkle remaining seeds (and seasoning, if used) over the top.

Bake at 200°C/400°F/Gas Mark 6 for 35–45 minutes or until slices have yellowed and shrunk slightly and feel dryish to the touch. Turn off heat and allow the plantains to cool in the oven. Peel off and discard the skin.

Serve in bowls as appetizers or as accompaniments to any savoury course.

NORIMAKI SUSHI

HERE IS a simplified, vegetarian version of Japanese Sushi to divert guests and test your dexterity. The seaweed called Nori is available ready-prepared in thin, pliable sheets from Japanese and Oriental specialist food stores, delicatessens and certain wholefood shops. Wasabi, fiery Japanese horseradish, shoyu and glutinous rice can also be found in such stores. Substitutions and omissions can be made but it is fun to try to learn about the real thing, though in Japan 'dashi' (tuna-flavoured stock) would be used, not vegetable stock.

————— SERVES 4–8 —————

225 g (8 oz) Japanese glutinous rice (or shortgrain pudding rice)
750 ml (1¼ pints) vegetable stock
2.5 ml (½ level tsp) sea salt
30 ml (2 tbsp) mirin (or sweet sherry)
30 ml (2 tbsp) shoyu (or soy) sauce
30 ml (2 tbsp) rice vinegar (or white wine vinegar)
6 20 cm (8 inch) squares of Nori (seaweed in sheets)

FILLINGS:
½ cucumber, peeled, cut into 1 × 1 cm (½ × ½ inch) pieces
1 sweet red pepper seeded, stem removed, sliced into 1 cm (½ inch) strips

TO SERVE:
alfalfa (or bean) sprouts
4 spring onions, sliced at both ends into fans (placed in iced water)

Put the dry rice into a heavy-based pan with the stock and sea salt. Bring to the boil. Cover, then reduce heat and leave to cook for 15–18/18–20 minutes or until soft and sticky.

Sprinkle over the sherry, shoyu and vinegar. Leave the pan uncovered and stand it in iced water to cool.

Spread 4 of the 8 sheets of Nori on a cloth or cling film. Stir and divide up the rice and cover one third of each sheet of Nori in an even rectangle to one long edge. Put a central core of cucumber down the length of two of these, and a central core of pepper down the length of the other two.

Starting from a long rice-covered edge roll up each parcel neatly and firmly to make a long baton, using the free edge of Nori to enclose the rest, every time. You will end with 4 batons. Line them up and using an oiled and very sharp serrated knife, cut each into 5 or 6, giving 20 or 24 little drums.

With the remaining rice make 8 balls. Cut each square of Nori into 4, making 8. Put rice and the garnishes (diced this time) into the squares and pull up the edges of each square, twisting to make purse shapes, opening out the frills, or else roll up into a roll, and twist the empty unfilled ends to form bonbons shapes. (Alternatively make both of the latter, so that there are 3 different shapes.) Chill. Any leftover rice should be rolled into firm balls.

Garnish a serving plate with a border of alfalfa sprouts. Set the Norimaki amongst these. Garnish with spring onion fans. Serve with accompanying seasonings (e.g. Polyglot Hot Seasoning or 'Seaweed Greens' Seasoning (pages 38 and 39)) and shoyu, or chilli paste or wasabi, the traditional accompaniment make this hot green horseradish paste (by adding a little water to the powder).

VOUTIRO KOUKOUNARIA

(Pine nut purée)

ONE AUTUMN some years ago on the island of Anghistri in Greece, I lay on warm rocks and idly extracted the pearly kernels from the pine cones. It was the first time I had seen or tasted pine nuts, and they were one of the final pleasures of a long and happy day. The scented warmth of island Greece always returns to me whenever I use them in my cooking. This recipe, a pure invention, is a tawny purée, cream or 'butter' which may be used as dip, spread, filling or snack.

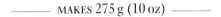

——— MAKES 275 g (10 oz) ———

225 g (8 oz) fresh pine nuts (pine kernels)
30 ml (2 level tbsp) Greek Hymettus honey
50 ml (2 fl oz) boiling water

1.25 ml ($\frac{1}{4}$ level tsp) sea salt (optional)
15–30 ml (1–2 tbsp) Greek Metaxa
   brandy (or other fruity brandy)

Dry roast half of the pine nuts in a clean, dry, heavy-based pan over moderate heat, shaking regularly to protect from uneven scorching. (They should become an even golden brown.)

Blend or crush the toasted and untoasted nuts with the honey to a thick paste. Dribble in the water gradually (so that the mixture retains its creaminess) until the required consistency is reached. Push down the mixture from the sides of the bowl at regular intervals. Taste, and add salt to taste for extra 'bite' and savoury balance.

Incorporate the brandy gradually to make a smooth purée. (Spooning or spreading consistency—the choice is yours).

Pack into a sterilized pot, jar or glass (preferably one with a non-metal lid) and store in the refrigerator. The surface tends to darken on standing.

Use as a spread, in place of butter on crusty, toasted, or oven-dried bread (called paximathia *in Greece), with warmed brioches or hot croissants—or perhaps, with good, black coffee and a Metaxa brandy, for an occasional treat.*

23

FISTIKIA VOUTIRO

(Pistachio purée with Pernod)

FOR ME, this recipe summons up Mediterranean warmth, colour, liveliness and sparkle. I feel that pistachios are too often relegated to studding quenelles or terrines, decorating ice creams and lending spurious flavour to desserts, (there are many false 'chopped pistachios' (almonds dyed green) and 'essences'). Although good pistachios now come from many parts of the world, southern Europe, the United States, and particularly the Middle East, there is great variation in size, colour, taste and treatment before we buy them. Some are vacuum packed, but for me, the best are those from Greek, Cypriot and Italian growers. (Discover them in delicatessens, packaged in cellophane, fresh from their place of origin.) I like best those nuts which have been rolled in lemon juice and salt and dried in the Mediterranean sunshine on Greek hillsides.

——— MAKES 275 g (10 oz) ———

225 g (8 oz) pistachio nuts freshly shelled, preferably salted (or 450 g (1 lb) in the shell)
50 g (2 oz) salted butter, at room temperature
freshly ground black pepper

30 ml (2 tbsp) Pernod, Ouzo, Raki or Ricard
salt (to taste)
boiling water or stock or heated fresh lemon juice (optional)

Remove (rub off between two palms) the mauve or purple skins from the shelled pistachios. Chop roughly, then pound, blend or crush the nuts (8–10 bursts of a food processor). Add small squares of the butter, pepper and liquor. Process to a rough, green paste. Taste, adjust seasonings (if you have used unsalted nuts you may require some salt). To this delicious creation may be added a little boiling water, stock or heated lemon juice to achieve a good consistency.

Cool, chill and pack into a sterilized pot (or several little pots) or into small jars (preferably with non-metal lids). Store in the refrigerator.

*U*se as a spread, a dip, a purée/filling for foods, on cooked vegetables, (with herbs),
or simply on a piece of good, crusty bread or toast. Serve with a little glass of aniseed liquor,
iced water or coffee (or all three).

LIPTOI FELLEGI

THE MOST interesting occasion on which I tasted Liptauer (or Liptoi) was with a Hungarian-born Canadian food enthusiast at the Gay Hussar in London's Soho. Instead of dessert I opted for the Liptoi. Because no serving suggestions were forthcoming and because I had imbibed the equivalent of quite a number of Puttonyos, I recklessly called for strawberries to accompany it. The Liptoi arrived, with crisp celery (far more logical) and good dark bread! Even so I enjoyed my frivolous berries and devoured the lot with considerable gusto.

———— SERVES 4 ————

125 g (4 oz) full fat cream cheese
125 g (4 oz) curd cheese
125 g (4 oz) salted butter
1 clove garlic, skinned and mashed
15 ml (1 level tbsp) Hungarian paprika
5 ml (1 level tsp) dry, hot mustard
10 ml (2 level tsp) caraway or dill seeds

TO SERVE:
crisp celery sticks and fresh radishes, in iced water
rye bread or other black bread, or else small crisp biscuits

In a bowl combine the 2 cheeses with the butter, until evenly blended. Work in the garlic, paprika, mustard and seeds, until the mixture is of a uniform consistency. Pile into a glass or silver dish. Arrange celery sticks and radishes. If you are feeling reckless have a bowl of strawberries of cherries nearby.

25

MODEL STARTS AND MODISH SNACKS

MARGARET PAYNE'S PORRIDGE

MY MOTHER'S breakfasts have always been, and still are a grand part of the remembered mosaic of my life, my childhood well-being. In summer we began with fresh fruit or home-preserved fruit in syrup. In winter we often began with porridge. Then came a good, protein-high course often reflecting seasonal specialties: eggs from our bantam hens, whitebait fritters, crumbed brains and plum sauce, smoked cod with parsley sauce, liver, kidney or mushrooms with frilly bacon. To finish we had toast and marmalade, then a hot milky beverage and tea or coffee for my father. Another treat of my mother's (especially if we felt forlorn) was to grate whole apples, skin, core and all and top this with a sprinkling of spice and a little sugar, to be eaten while it still had that vitamin-fresh taste. In this recipe I have combined two of her breakfast ideas. Even Digby Anderson, the *Spectator*'s champion of decent breakfasts, might well approve!

──────── SERVES 4 ────────

50 g (2 oz) flaked or roasted unblanched
   almonds, roughly chopped
75 g (3 oz) traditional, medium Scottish
   oatmeal
15 g ($\frac{1}{2}$ oz) wheatgerm
5 ml (1 level tsp) salt
boiling water

TO SERVE:
1 crisp apple
molasses (or Barbados sugar) sugar
ground mixed spice (optional)
icy-cold fresh cream, soured cream, crème
   fraiche or natural yogurt

Put the almonds and oatmeal into a medium, heavy-based saucepan with the wheatgerm, salt and boiling water, stirring with a wooden spoon all the time. Cook over gentle heat until simmering, reduce heat and cook, uncovered, stirring now and then, until the mixture becomes opaque and aromatic and as thick as you like it (long cooking will evaporate off more liquid and make it become more thick).

Pour into 4 plates or bowls. Grate some apple (all but the stalk) directly over the centre of each serving. Sprinkle with sugar (and mixed spice, if liked). Serve accompanied by a 'lagoon' of the dairy product of your choice. Delicious!

PERSONALIZED SNACK MUESLI

WHY BUY muesli when you can make your own recipe, virtually to order, packed full of known, delicious and high-class ingredients? What is more, it is harmless fun to make at the weekend for the coming week or fortnight. This recipe is absolutely delicious and encourages the most difficult of eaters to participate at breakfast (or indeed any other) time. It is a snack food as far as I am concerned. Encourage children and teenagers to make it—a really positive and educational contribution, for it requires intelligent shopping and selection as well as cooking. Go to a good wholefood supplier and learn about seeds, nuts, unprocessed cereals, unsulphured dried fruit and all the different types of sugar. The world is there in your kitchen!

———— MAKES 1.6 kg (3½ lb) ————

75 g (3 oz) molasses sugar (or Barbados sugar)
50 g (2 oz) molasses (or black treacle)
100 g (4 oz) pure malt extract, or liquid honey
30 ml (2 tbsp) fruity olive oil, or safflower oil
30 ml (2 tbsp) freshly squeezed orange, lemon or lime juice
400 g (14 oz) jumbo (minimally processed) oats
125 g (4 oz) wheatgerm

50 g (2 oz) toasted sesame seeds
50 g (2 oz) alfalfa seeds (or sunflower seeds)
50 g (2 oz) desiccated coconut, plain or toasted
400 g (14 oz) sun-dried, sharp-flavoured apricots, chopped
125 g (4 oz) seedless raisins
125 g (4 oz) dried prunes or figs, chopped
125 g (4 oz) unsalted, shelled nuts, (hazels, pecans, pistachios or Brazils) chopped coarsely

27

Heat the sugar, molasses, malt, oil and juice together in a large heavy-based saucepan for 4–5 minutes until thick, bubbling and toffee-like (a little should form a soft ball in cold water). Measure out and mix the oats, wheatgerm, seeds and coconut. Add them, all at once, to the malted mixture. Stir to coat them, working quite quickly and energetically.

While still hot, smooth out the mixture on to 2 large paper-lined roasting pans. Dry the muesli in the centre of a 200°C/400°F/Gas Mark 6 oven for 30 minutes. Halfway through cooking, stir from the edges to centre, and vice versa, changing the shelf positions of each tray at the same time.

Break up the mixture and allow it to cool. Pack into 1 or 2 large jars, scattering the raisins, chopped fruit and nuts evenly throughout. Use with the dairy product (milk, cream, yogurt, fromage blanc, fromage frais or crème fraîche) of your choice.

EGGS MENAGE A TROIS

(Illustrated facing page 64)

FOR THIS you will need 4 pretty bowls packed with rock salt, or 12 egg cups or 12 small glasses for the eggs. The recipe consists of 3 different treatments for soft-boiled eggs, though variations are possible. I first tasted this concept at Antony Worral-Thompson's restaurant in London's Beauchamp Place: it was a delight. (He used mousses of salmon, for example, and topped his eggs with such delicacies as Beluga caviar—utterly delicious.) Soft-cooked eggs are stirred with butter or cream and added flavourings: it is scarcely a new idea—but the presentation elevates the dish. Enjoy this on a leisurely weekend morning for a late breakfast or brunch. It also makes a substantial starter course to a light supper. Get all the ingredients and egg dishes ready before you begin.

Some experts say that good wine is spoiled by egg but I feel that an elegant fresh fruit or vegetable juice 'cocktail' (especially one made using a juicer), a 'spritzer' of peach juice and mineral water, or for evenings, a crisp but flowery Sauvignon or a Juliénas would still be acceptable (or of course some non-vintage dry champagne for sheer frivolity's sake).

———— SERVES 4 ————

12 small free range eggs, at room temperature
25 g (1 oz) butter
25 g (1 oz) fromage blanc battu
2.5 ml (½ level tsp) salt
freshly ground black pepper
30 ml (2 level tbsp) chopped chives or parsley

TOPPINGS:
40 ml (8 level tsp) Tapénaro (see page 20) or ready made Tapénade (olive paste)

40 ml (8 level tsp) Seaweed Seasoning (see page 39)
40 ml (8 level tsp) Pestle Sauce (see page 50) or freshly made pesto
1 head red oak leaf lettuce (feuilles de chêne)
8 leaves pale curly endive (frisée)— optional
8 small slices good bread (or 4 large slices)

Put the eggs (at room temperature) into simmering salted water and bring gently back to boiling point. Simmer for 1 minute then cover, turn off heat and leave for 4–5 minutes. Test one for readiness: when the top is removed the white is firm but the yolk is still soft and runny at centre. Remove eggs and cool rapidly under running cold water.

Remove the narrow, pointed tops from the eggs and scoop out the soft egg. Mash roughly with a knife and add the butter, fromage blanc battu, salt, pepper and parsley or chives. Check seasonings.

Wrap 1 or 2 pretty red lettuce leaves around each egg shell and stand in the salt in the bowls or in the egg cups or glasses. (Make sure that shells are wiped clean, though jagged shell edges are part of the charm.) The lettuce should appear to make a frill around the top of each.

Spoon enough egg mixture into each egg to come to within 0.5 cm (¼ inch) of the top. (Use any egg left over in sandwiches, etc.)

Spoon 10 ml (2 level tsp) olive paste neatly on top of 4 eggs, working gently so that the top surface of egg is hidden. Top the remaining 8 eggs with Seaweed Seasoning and basil sauce in the same way. Tuck some frisée between the containers, if wished.

Toast slices of bread and cut into fingers for dipping.

Serve while the eggs are still warm and the toast crisp. (Alternatively, the eggs can be prepared well in advance and chilled and toppings and toast done at the last minute.)

OEUFS PASTOUCHE

THE NAME of this recipe is itself a pastiche of the names Babouche and Pasta, and it is a distant relation of an Alice B. Toklas idea. The soft egg yolks, when cut through, flow in a golden stream making excellent crusty bread an essential accompaniment. A charming, eclectic breakfast, brunch, lunch or supper dish or appetizer. Use leftover green pasta if you have it. The cheese and olives are more suited for lunch or supper than for breakfast or brunch (they do, however, give great interest to the dish). A pretty and decorative start to any day, and sustaining enough for you to make lunch a rather light affair—useful when you are busy.

———— SERVES 4 ————

29

2 large 450 g (1 lb) total weight marmande
   (beefsteak) tomatoes
25 g (1 oz) cooked, drained green pasta
   noodles (tagliarini)
25 g (1 oz) Brie, Savarin or Coulommiers
   cheese (optional)
4 black Niçoise olives, stoned and chopped
   (optional)

4 size 5 or 6 eggs, at room temperature
60 ml (4 level tbsp) crème fraîche
1.25 ml ($\frac{1}{4}$ tsp) saffron strands, or
   powdered pure saffron
8 chive stalks, halved (optional)

TO SERVE:
crusty bread

Halve the tomatoes crossways, scoop out and remove the central pulp and flesh, leaving the walls intact. Drain, upside down, using absorbent kitchen paper.

Chop the pasta and spoon into the cases. (Add the cheese and chopped olives if this is liked, otherwise leave it simple.)

Position 5 cm (2 inches) beneath a preheated grill and cook gently for 6–7 minutes or until the cases are hot (and the cheese, if used, is bubbling). While the tomatoes are cooking, cover the eggs with near boiling water in a medium pan and gently boil for 5–6 minutes. Cool quickly and briefly under cold water, carefully shell the hot eggs and place one lengthways inside each case. Spoon over the crème fraîche, sprinkle some saffron on to each then replace under the grill and grill on high for a further 1–1$\frac{1}{2}$ minutes.

Add a garnish of chives, if liked, and serve these little delicacies with the bread of your choice.

CHAMPAGNE QUAILS' EGG BRUNCH

T HE CHAMPAGNE vinegar required in this recipe is exquisite but expensive, so rather than discard the pickle liquor, boil it again and re-use if wished. Although they must be prepared at least a day in advance, the presentation of these eggs makes them pretty enough to grace any Easter celebration lunch, or indeed to enhance any brunch, lunch or cocktail party table. Have a bowl of rock salt near at hand for those who like it, together with some homemade lemon mayonnaise.

——— SERVES 4–8 ———

*48 (4 dozen) fresh quails' eggs, at room
   temperature*

PICKLING LIQUID:
*300 ml ($\frac{1}{2}$ pint) Champagne or white wine
   vinegar*
300 ml ($\frac{1}{2}$ pint) Muscadet or Chablis
150 ml ($\frac{1}{4}$ pint) water
20 ml (4 tsp) pickling spice
*4 dried fennel, thyme or oregano stalks,
   halved*

TO SERVE:
$\frac{1}{2}$ head of curly endive (frisée) optional
sea salt (optional)
lemon mayonnaise (optional)
good crisp-textured bread

Hard boil the eggs, covering them with cold water and bringing them to a gentle boil for 5 minutes (depending on size). Cool them quickly under cold running water. When quite cold, shell the eggs.

Combine the pickle ingredients in a non-metal pan and boil for 2 minutes. Pack the shelled eggs into a 1 litre ($1\frac{3}{4}$ pints) sterilized glass or china jar or pot. Pour over enough of the hot pickling liquid to fill the jar, pushing the fennel stalks well down between the eggs. Cover with seal, lid or cling film and refrigerate for 1–6 days. (Flavours develop with time though even 1 day is adequate.)

Strain the eggs (reserving the liquid), and pile them into the centre of a shallow dish. Scatter over the spices and stalks. Surround the eggs with a frill of curly green and yellow leaves. Serve with salt, mayonnaise and bread.

GARNISHED EGGS ECHIRE

ECHIRE BUTTER, I was once proudly informed, is considered the best butter in France, maybe the world. I first tasted it in a Paris bistro à vin in the 14th arrondissement. It was a tiny bar run by a sensible man who served merely freshly made sandwiches on Poilâne bread (another triumph) with cured ham, rillettes or good cheese. The taste of the butter was memorable, however, and I began seeing its proud gold and blue rosettes in épiceries, grand restaurants and good markets.

In the following recipe it is good butter which distinguishes the dish, along with, of course, very fresh eggs and a pretty, tasty garnish. Muffins are served at the side. The secret here lies in having the garnishes already prepared and hot, the muffins crusty and heated plates ready. The eggs continue cooking on the plate so they must really be moist on top when served.

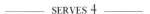

SERVES 4

8 medium-large fresh eggs (preferably farm eggs)
2.5 ml (½ level tsp) salt
freshly, coarsely-ground or crushed white pepper (mignonette)
30 ml (2 tbsp) Muscadet or other dry white wine
50 g (2 oz) Echiré butter (or other good slightly salted butter)
4 granary or wholemeal muffins, split

GARNISHES (choose one of the following):
25 g (1 oz) jets de houblon (hop shoots) or
    25 g (1 oz) nettle tips (blanched, drained and sautéed in échiré), or
    25 g (1 oz) dandelion leaves (blanched, drained and sautéed in échiré) or
    50 g (2 oz) asparagus trimmings (blanched, drained, sautéed in échiré) or
    100 g (4 oz) sea kale, stems and leaves (sautéed in échiré) or 100 g (4 oz) red pepper rings, seeded and halved (sautéed in échiré)

Steam the garnish of your choice. Either use a steamer basket over boiling water or a pierced metal colander or throw thoroughly wetted food, finely sliced, into a hot non-stick pan, cover with a lid, and shake over heat until cooked. Add a knob of échiré to the drained garnish and keep gently hot.

Toast the muffins and keep them warm.

Heat a large, heavy omelette pan. Whisk the eggs with the salt, pepper and wine, using a fork, until they are barely mixed.

Add the butter to the heated pan, tilting it until it foams, and the sides and base are well covered.

Pour the eggs into the pan, reduce the heat and gently push the eggs into 'ruches' in the pan as each part cooks, never allowing any unevenness to occur, and using a flat-sided wooden spatula or other blunt tool.

Remove the toasted muffins to heated plates, stacking one slightly upon the other and placing to one side.

Spoon the creamy, barely set (baveuse) eggs (still liquid on top) on to each plate and add the little garnishes. Proffer extra pepper, for those who enjoy it.

LIVELY LOAVES

CRUSTY GRIGNON GENOAS

THESE SAIL-SHAPED chunks of French bread, 'designer cut' to give attractive and crisped surfaces, are excellent to use alone, or as hot crusts to dip into purées of root vegetables, chickpeas and beans, tomato or other fresh sauces, or with a spreading of Pestle Sauce (see page 50), Tapénaro (see page 20) or simply to dunk into a huge bowl of Pestle Soup (see page 50) or other hearty soup. They are also good to serve guests if for any reason the wine is opened and the glasses are filled, the guests are hungry but the meal is not yet ready! Use granary sticks or traditional long French baguettes or flutes, though the brown bread, in this instance, has the greater charm.

———— SERVES 4–8 ————

1 long stick of fresh bread (granary or
    French)
1 garlic clove, halved and crushed
30 ml (2 tbsp) pure virgin olive oil
freshly ground black pepper

TO SERVE:
fresh herbs

Cut off the 2 ends of the loaf at right angles and keep them. Cutting first at 45° (diagonal) then crossways, (at right angles) to the loaf, cut it into 10 (or so) tubby 'triangles'.

Slide a sharp knife almost through from the smallest angled point and split open each piece. (It will resemble a boat's sail (e.g. a genoa). Keep each pair of 'sails' joined.)

Stir the crushed garlic into the oil and paint it quickly over the cut surfaces of the 12 bread pieces. Scatter with herbs.

Brown the grignons briefly on a tray in the oven 230°C/450°F/Gas Mark 8 for 8–12 minutes or until crusty. Eat the bread while it is still hot.

CLOCKWISE FROM THE TOP: EFFIE'S GREEN SPRING SOUP (PAGE 57) SOUP
MANGE-CLOUD (PAGE 49) AND DORIS-ROSA JELLIED SOUP (PAGE 55), MELON, CARROT AND TOMATO SOUP (PAGE 59)

CHEESE, DRIED TOMATO AND HERB LOAF

THIS LOAF is very quick to make. It has considerable flavour: enough to make the bread itself the substance of the brunch, lunch, snack or revellers' midnight breakfast. This amenable bread has many uses: with good butter or soft cheese, fresh fruit or preserves or pickles. A glass of beer, wine, or cup of coffee or tea, all make suitable beverages to accompany it. Dried tomato is a unique product: sun-dried then packed in oil, it is flavourful, wine-red and superb. No other food equals it, though prune (when tried as a substitute) was good but made a damp dough. Good ingredients invariably produce interesting results. Italian delicatessens often stock this delicious food, loose or in jars.

MAKES 450 g (1 lb LOAF)
SERVES 4

25 g (1 oz) cold, coarsely grated butter
225 g (8 oz) self-raising flour
10 ml (2 level tsp) baking powder
2.5 ml ($\frac{1}{2}$ level tsp) salt
25 g (1 oz) fresh Parmesan or Romano cheese, grated
50 g (2 oz) dried Italian tomatoes in oil, drained, well-dried and chopped

30 ml (2 level tbsp) chopped parsley
50 ml (2 fl oz) milk

GLAZE:
30 ml (2 level tbsp) honey
15 ml (1 level tbsp) fresh Parmesan or Romano cheese, grated

Stir all the ingredients, except the milk, together until blended. Make a well and pour in the milk all at once. Stir quickly to form a dough.

Knead a little in the bowl to form a compact ball. Pat out on a prepared baking sheet to a 20 cm (8 inch) circle. Mark into 6 or 8 segments.

Bake in an oven at 200°C/400°F/Gas Mark 6 for 20 minutes or until crusty and hollow-sounding when tapped. Eat, thickly sliced, while the bread is warm.

33

ASSORTED HOMEMADE PASTA. CLOCKWISE FROM THE TOP: FRESH
ORANGE-ZESTED FETTUCINE (PAGES 76–77), CARDOMOM AND SAFFRON PASTA (PAGES 70–71), MOREL AND
PARMIGIANO PASTA (PAGES 78–79), PURSLANE AND PARSLEY FETTUCINE (PAGES 80–81)

SEEDED SPINACH COB OR PLAIT LOAF

MANY PEOPLE avoid breadmaking because it seems too difficult or too long. Using today's micronized yeast (not granules, but fine powdered yeast, available in sachets, which may or may not contain Vitamin C), any breadmaking becomes more like scone-making. The dry yeast is sprinkled into the dry ingredients as if it were baking powder. Here is a loaf which is effortless, especially if the rising instructions (simple but effective) are followed exactly.

——— MAKES 550 g (1¼ lb) LOAF ———

*25 g (1 oz) cooked, dried and chopped
  spinach, (from 50 g (2 oz) fresh)*
*300 g (11 oz) wholemeal (wholewheat)
  flour*
*12.5 ml (2½ level tsp) micronized yeast, or
  half of one sachet of dried yeast*
5 ml (1 level tsp) salt

30 ml (2 level tbsp) sugar
30 ml (2 level tbsp) blue poppy seeds
225 ml (8 fl oz) lukewarm water

GLAZE:
1 egg, beaten

Wash and cook the spinach (leaving the washing water clinging), until barely tender and bright green. Squeeze dry and chop.

Mix the flour, yeast, salt, sugar, seeds and spinach in a large bowl. Stir in the water all at once to make a firm dough.

Knead for 5 minutes or until satiny smooth. Put into an oiled bowl, cover with plastic wrap and stand on a rack over hot water for 30–45 minutes or until doubled in bulk. Punch down the dough.

Shape dough to form a perfect round cob. (Alternatively, roll the dough into a rectangle, slash twice and plait the 3 strands into 1 plait, securing ends firmly.)

Put on to an oiled baking sheet. Cover with plastic and stand on a rack over hot water for 25–30 minutes or until again increased in volume.

Lightly brush with egg, bake towards top of an oven at 200°C/400°F/Gas Mark 6 for about 30 minutes. Tap the base to see if the dough sounds hollow. It should be crusty. Serve warm with quark, Liptoi (see page 25) or triple cream cheese or as the basis of an open sandwich. It is also good briefly toasted. The plait is best served untoasted, pulled into curved pieces.

Zaffymec Horseshoe Brioche

(Illustrated facing page 64)

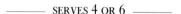

THIS GOLDEN bread, in the shape of a lucky horseshoe, is wickedly high in cholesterol but enchanting for special treats. Only make it for the appreciative— not the dyspeptic, the allergenic, the dieter. Its smell scents the whole kitchen towards the end of cooking time. Although rich, it is a dough best eaten the same day. It seems luxurious for the amount (not large) of effort expended and would grace any table. It can be used as sweet or savoury bread.

——— SERVES 4 OR 6 ———

450 g (1 lb) unbleached white flour
5 ml (1 level tsp) salt
10 ml (2 level tsp) caster sugar
2.5 ml (½ level tsp) dried micronized yeast
  ('easyblend' or 'easybake')
1.25 ml (1 sachet) powdered pure saffron

125 ml (4 fl oz) milk, scalded then cooled
  to lukewarm
3 large eggs beaten (keep a little aside
  for glaze)
150 g (5 oz) butter, chopped into 24 pieces

Sift the flour, salt, sugar, yeast and powdered saffron into the bowl of a food processor. Add the lukewarm milk beaten with the eggs and using the dough hook, process in 6 or 8 bursts, to make a soft sticky dough.

Add half the butter, process in several longish bursts until well incorporated. Add the remaining butter, repeat process, then remove to a floured surface and knead by hand for 2–3 minutes until the dough becomes velvety and elastic. Put into an oiled bowl and leave in a warm, damp place (such as on a rack over hand-hot water) for 40 minutes or until doubled in bulk.

Punch down, then roll out the dough to a 30 cm (12 inch) circle. Roll it up into a loose tube, then draw ends together to meet, forming a horse-shoe shape. Slash well on the diagonal about 6 or 8 times, to a depth of 2 cm (¾ inch). Cover loosely and refrigerate for a second and slower rising (near the top of a refrigerator, not the coldest part) for 3 hours, or overnight, if preferred.

Brush the loaf with the reserved egg glaze and bake at 190°C/375°F/Gas Mark 5 for 45–50 minutes, or until light, airy, aromatic, golden and crusty.

*S*erve the brioche warm, sliced thickly and with extra butter, (naughty but
wonderful) with any of the following: honey, preserves, nut spreads, or crème fraîche.
It may be used to accompany any main dish (sweet or savoury) or just cheer up the day!

AMAZING TASTES

MALAY OMELETTE GARNISH

THIS TYPE of rolled omelette garnish is commonly served with rice or noodle dishes in Malaysia, but it can be used to good effect as a garnish for any food lacking protein or in need of texture and taste contrast.

You can, of course, add your own variations when it comes to flavouring the egg mixture. Add very finely chopped herbs such as dill, parsley, tarragon or fresh coriander; or you could include some diced green, red, yellow or black peppers—whatever will offset the colourings of the dish to be garnished. The omelette can always be prepared well ahead of time and used as a last minute garnish to liven up a dish.

——— SERVES 4–6 ———

10 ml (2 tsp) groundnut (peanut or arachide) oil
1–2 small fresh red chillies, seeded, finely sliced
1 spring onion, sliced crossways (white and green parts)

3 medium-large eggs, lightly beaten
15 ml (1 tbsp) vegetable stock or water

TO SERVE:
crisp salad leaves

Heat the oil in a large 20 cm (8 inch)-diameter heavy-based pan until very hot.

Put the chillies, spring onion, eggs and stock into a bowl and beat until blended. Pour the omelette mixture into the hot pan. Cook over fierce heat without stirring, until the omelette has set.

Slide the omelette out of the pan. Roll it up (browned surface showing) into a tight cylinder. Slice it into tiny, decorative spirals. Heap on a bed of salad leaves. The omelette spirals are sprinkled over rice, noodles, legumes, potatoes, root vegetable dishes or salads.

SEED, NUT AND HERB CITRUS SEASONING

THIS HOMEMADE condiment may be used to season food in place of salt or as an additional 'flavour enhancer' made from delicious, known ingredients. Keep it on the table in a small dish, and supply a mustard spoon for serving. This seasoning will make simply-cooked vegetables, baked potatoes, open sandwiches, pasta, rice dishes and legumes taste lively and altogether different. Use it sparingly, however, for any 'salt' can lose its savour if overused.

———— MAKES 275 g (10 oz) ————

175 g (6 oz) sesame seeds
30 ml (2 tbsp) dried salted black beans
15 ml (1 level tbsp) freshly shredded orange zest
5 ml (1 level tsp) freshly shredded lime zest
15 ml (1 level tbsp) dried orange flower 'petales' or 'boutons'

5 ml dried lemon scented verbena (verveine) optional
50 g (2 oz) roasted, salted, cashew nuts, roughly chopped
50 g (2 oz) shelled pecan nuts, roughly chopped
5 ml (1 tsp) citric acid or tartaric acid

Put the sesame seeds into a large heavy-based frying pan over a moderate heat. Stir constantly until there is an aromatic smell and the seeds are golden brown—about 4 minutes.

Put one sixth of all the hot seeds into an electric grinder, with the beans, the 2 zests, and the dried orange flowers/buds, and the verbena (if used).

Grind, in short bursts, to a coarse powder. Repeat the process until all ingredients have been used (apart from some sesame seeds). Add the remaining third of unground sesame seeds to the mixture and the citric (or tartaric) acid.

Leave the powder to cool completely uncovered. When cold, pack into china pots or dark glass jars. Seal, label and store in a cool dark dry place.

POLYGLOT HOT SEASONING

IN THE old tradition of 'poudre fort' or 'poudre blanche', this mixed pepper-type seasoning is used instead of normal ground black or white pepper at the table, or in cooking. It contains dried white, green and pink peppercorns, if you can find them. (A quite unjustified 'scare' put them off the market shelves some time ago, but they have since been declared safe once more now that the confusion about their provenance is over.) Red chillies, crushed juniper and allspice berries are also used in the seasoning. It is curious and interesting. To reduce the hotness some nuts are also added, which create balanced flavour.

———— MAKES 125 g (4 oz) ————

25 g (1 oz) green peppercorns
25 g (1 oz) pink or black peppercorns
25 g (1 oz) white peppercorns
2 dried red chillies, seeds removed

15 ml (1 level tbsp) juniper berries
15 ml (1 level tbsp) allspice berries
50 g (2 oz) dry roasted, salted almonds, chopped

Using only a quarter measure of each ingredient at a time, grind them to a rough powder.

Repeat this process until all the ingredients are ground. Store the seasoning in an airtight container in a cool dark place.

U se this hot seasoning with all dishes which require extra piquancy.
It is particularly good with creamy purées of root vegetables,
soft cheese or stir-fried dishes.

'SEAWEED GREENS' SEASONING

I T IS fascinating to discover that the tasty cellophane-like 'seaweed' served in many oriental restaurants is actually deep-fried young cabbage greens. (If frying is done very accurately, very quickly and at the correct temperature, foods fried do *not* become fat saturated at all. The fat 'seals' the foods effectively.)

Serve it (alone, if wished) as an appetizer or with soup, or as an accompaniment for Oriental dishes. But for a really good seasoning, add the other ingredients, mixed in a small bowl or dish at the table, to use sprinkled over food in place of salt, for variety and for fun.

———— SERVES 4 ————

250 g (9 oz) spring greens
300 ml ($\frac{1}{2}$ pint) safflower, sunflower or groundnut (peanut or arachide) oil
50 g (2 oz) sunflower seeds
25 g (1 oz) sesame seeds

45 ml (3 tbsp) shoyu (soy) sauce
1.25 ml ($\frac{1}{4}$ level tsp) each of salt, pepper and sugar
5 ml (1 level tsp) chilli paste, if available, (or use ground chillies)

Hold heads of spring greens under running water, then shake very dry. Slice finely into 3 mm ($\frac{1}{8}$ inch) shreds using a sharp serrated knife.

Heat the oil in a deep pan, or wok, until it is very hot, almost 190°C/380°F (but not smoking). Deep fry half the cabbage greens at a time until the shreds have become translucent and crinkled. Remove the cabbage with a slotted spoon and drain on kitchen paper. Repeat the process with the second half of the cabbage greens. Allow to grow completely cold. Break up with the fingers.

Toss the 2 seeds in the shoyu. Spread out under a preheated grill on a layer of foil, so that they dry out. Grill, turning frequently until dark and crisp. Allow to cool.

Toss the seeds with salt, pepper, sugar and chilli seasonings, with the cabbage, at the table for people to nibble at, or use as a seasoning on many kinds of foods.

Soup Making and Stock Taking

THE DOUBLE-ENTENDRE in the title of this chapter is intentional. It does indeed imply that you should not merely resort to a stock cube each time you read the words 'vegetable stock', for this section contains some of the recipes which can most support my high-nutrient, balanced-calories but fresh-food emphasis.

While soup making will never become a lost art, I believe that it is certainly in need of a real re-examination. Many old stock and soup-making methods in other cook books suggest long hours of preparation and cooking time, even for all-vegetable soups and stocks which (unlike meat, poultry and game) frequently become aromatic, full-coloured and tasty within minutes, not hours. Furthermore, while in the past soups have functioned as 'fuel food' today that aspect is less of a priority. It therefore seemed important to me to provide some new, minimal but creative ways of giving recipes for stocks (and for soups) which could act as support-systems to many of the other clean, delicate or robustly flavoured dishes in this book. And if time, effort, energy and nutrients could be saved—then so much the better! Aroma, colour, consistency and temperature differences—these are what make soups so charming to us, so primal in their appeal.

INTERNATIONAL STOCKS

Because I enjoy travel and tastes of many continents I have tried to include a variety of types of stock—British and European-style stocks, an Asian-cum-Pacific one, a Polish-influenced stock, an Oriental stock (with very wide application) and an almost-instant (15 minutes to cook) stock. These mattered to me, tremendously. If I as an author could not tell you, the reader, a way to make delicious liquids for the start of your dishes, then what use in continuing?

But there is a hidden bonus—not only are many of these stocks delicious in their own right as natural liquid flavourings for many cooking uses (simmering, boiling, steaming, in sauces, casseroles, mousses and purées, for example) but, with a handful of additions they can be turned into brunch, lunch, supper and even main-course soups: hundreds of ideas are here based on very little effort.

Multi-purpose soups

Many of my soups perform dual or even triple functions. I have included some fruit soups, novelties not meant for everyday use. Some utilize the best of what the season's fruit provides, others are 10-minute masterpieces of culinary engineering! Some are almost 'solid' fruit juices, some nearly become dip or spread consistency when served chilled and others become rather like cocktails, depending upon how they are used and presented. Almost all include good-tasting juices, stocks, fresh herbs, often flavourful liquids such as wine, cider, or even, in one recipe, ginger ale! Ready-made ingredients are not common in my recipes, though purchased seasonings, sweeteners and flavourings (such as flower-scented waters—rose and citrus, as well as geranium flower water) feature. Read my introductions, serving suggestions and wine notes. The raw materials are carefully selected for taste, goodness and individual charm as well as the way they combine with each other.

As for the more robust recipes, a taste of community shows itself in the other soups—from the hearty Niçoise-style mixed vegetable Pestle Soup, to the purées, pastes and creams of ingredients which range from everyday red lentils or pumpkin, to a blend of artichokes, potato and mange-tout peas (there is even a soup with herb-speckled 'clouds' floating on top of the tureen). Mongolian Hot Pot is another 'people's' soup (Thai Fire Pot is another name for it), which bubbles away at the table for guests to cook and serve themselves from—what delights! My French Onion Soup is not classic at all but an original version inspired by a consummate cook and gourmand (in the proper sense), whose knowledge, balance and sense of humour has helped always to make cooking fun and worthwhile.

Many recipes from this section suggest where certain delicious, rare and unusual or difficult-to-obtain ingredients can be located. I live near to one of the world's most delightful (and justly famous) street markets, so I have an unfair advantage, perhaps. But to know what type of specialist supplier, delicatessen, stall, market or merchant sells each type of commodity is, at least, a start.

In many large and even medium-sized cities, towns, suburbs, you are unlikely not to find at least a handful of so-called ethnic food stores and the major supermarkets are becoming increasingly adventurous in their choice of fresh produce and variety of ingedients. Cultivate a good relationship with your local store keepers and stall-holders—much can be learned this way.

Soup making always reflects the flair, the imaginativeness and the individual style of the cook—no matter how simple the dish may be. It is an activity worthy of pleasure and regard.

41

ELEMENTAL STOCKS

SOLIDARITY SOUP STOCK

A CURIOUS JEWEL-LIKE red stock coloured and flavoured with raw beets, radishes, red wine and vinegar. Add new garnishes (barley, noodles, dumplings, extra cubed root vegetables, cabbage (red or green), brilliant rings of carrot and dill pickles could all appear) and it becomes the basis of a great 'mother soup'. Stir in soured cream, crème fraîche, fromage blanc battu or thick strained yogurt if wished: though this is best done at the table (or at least not before serving time). This soup can both enliven bleak winter days and be soothing on hot summer evenings.

The stock can be frozen or chilled although it is really delicious when newly made. Add herbs to serve.

If using as a more filling soup, retrieve, shred and add the beetroot and some of the radishes and the soup embellishments of your choice.

MAKES 750 ml ($1\frac{1}{4}$ pints)

SERVES 4

15 ml (1 tbsp) olive oil
225 g (8 oz) radishes, topped, tailed and
    sliced thickly
350 g (12 oz) raw, baby beets, unpeeled,
    topped, tailed and sliced thickly
2 cloves garlic, peeled and crushed
50 g (2 oz) shallots or button onions,
    skinned and chopped
15 g ($\frac{1}{2}$ oz) dried wild mushrooms, (or
    ceps), crumbled
300 ml ($\frac{1}{2}$ pint) medium dry red wine

600 ml (1 pint) water
1 cinnamon stick, crushed
1 vanilla pod, split lengthways (optional)
15 ml (1 level tbsp) allspice berries,
    crushed
45 ml (3 tbsp) red wine vinegar
salt and freshly ground pepper

TO SERVE:
30 ml (2 level tbsp) fresh mint, coriander,
    lovage or flat leaf parsley leaves

Heat the oil in a large non-metal soup pan or other large, heavy-based, lidded pan. Sauté the sliced radish and beets for 2–3 minutes, stirring frequently.

Add garlic, shallots, mushrooms, red wine, water, and the 3 spices. Bring to boiling, point, cover, reduce the heat and simmer for 20–25 minutes, or until the beets are very tender. Taste, add vinegar to 'sharpen' the flavour as wished, and season carefully. Strain if the liquid is to be used as stock.

Saxon Vegetable Stock

Somehow, carrots, barley, fresh herbs, a touch of nutmeg and a dash of vinegar spell Saxon to my imagination (my knowledge of history is creatively poetical and instinctive, rather than accurate). Nonetheless, something historically English survives in this old-fashioned, homely stock. Although the barley tends to discolour the liquid and give a certain cloudiness, do not be disheartened: the goodness and taste are well worth trying.

This stock can be made into lovely winter soup when the cooked barley is replaced after straining, and new fresh vegetable garnishes are added. Be imaginative—use it frequently, but do not omit the vinegar, which is an essential part.

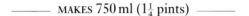

——— MAKES 750 ml ($1\frac{1}{4}$ pints) ———

1 large Spanish onion, skinned and quartered
8 cloves
1 whole nutmeg
4 celery sticks, chopped
2 carrots, skinned and chopped
25 g (1 oz) pot barley or pearl barley, (soaked overnight and drained)

8 white peppercorns
fresh bouquet garni (sage, thyme, parsley stalks and bay)
1.1 litres (2 pints) water
5–7.5 ml (1–1$\frac{1}{2}$ level tsp) rock or sea salt
50 g (2 oz) chopped fresh parsley
15 ml (1 tbsp) wine vinegar

Pull the quartered onion apart into 8 pieces and stick each part with a clove. Put these, with the nutmeg, celery, carrots, pre-soaked barley, peppercorns, fresh herbs and water into a large soup pan, flameproof lidded pan or casserole.

Bring to the boil, (about 10 minutes). Reduce heat to simmer, cover and leave to cook for 30 minutes. Add the chopped parsley, another 150 ml ($\frac{1}{4}$ pint) water and cook, covered, for a further 15 minutes. (Top up the liquid even more if necessary—barley is a thirsty grain!)

Strain, pressing out liquid thoroughly, taste and add salt as required, and a little vinegar to 'sharpen' the taste. Use immediately as stock or soup, or freeze or refrigerate for later use as cooking stock. Some or all of the barley is pleasant to include, when used for soup.

——— VARIATIONS ———

Small cubes of one component vegetable (e.g. carrot) and some finely cut vegetable such as baby turnips, green beans or shelled fresh peas.

A handful of mange-tout peas, some green leek rings, finely shredded, and a dash of cream.

Field or button mushrooms, sliced, shredded cabbage or sprouts, and long grain rice or ground or flaked almonds.

43

EUROPEAN SOUP STOCK

THIS PLEASANTLY clear, mellow stock has some sweetness and more than a suggestion of aniseed to it. The colour is golden and would become more pronounced if zest of an orange (in place of a lemon) were to be added. This stock gives a stylish unobtrusive taste. Use it as an everyday cooking stock in place of stock cubes, or dress it up with some fresh garnishings (as suggested) or by adding some more of its component ingredients, (but raw) towards serving time, keeping them finely cut to retain their charm. The addition of wine or dry cider added towards the end is pleasant but not essential and contributes extra volume and body.

MAKES 750 ml (1¼ pints)

SERVES 4

2 cloves garlic, crushed
4–6 shallots, skinned and quartered
225 g (8 oz) or 1 large, leek, sliced
225 g (8 oz), or 1, Spanish onion, skinned and sliced
fresh bouquet garni (parsley stalks, fresh bay, celery and thyme sprigs)

15 cm (6 inch) lemon or orange zest
1 large carrot, scrubbed and chopped
1 large head fennel, scrubbed and quartered
10–15 white peppercorns
1.1 litres (2 pints) water
150 ml (¼ pint) dry white wine or cider
5–7.5 ml (1–1½ level tsp) sea or rock salt

Put all the ingredients, except the wine and sea salt into a large soup pan, flameproof lidded pan or casserole. Add the water and bring to the boil, (about 10 minutes). Reduce heat to simmer, cover and leave to cook for about 40–45 minutes. Add the wine or cider and leave to cook a little longer, uncovered.

Strain the stock, pressing out liquids thoroughly. Taste and add salt as required, and some freshly ground pepper, if needed. Use immediately as stock or soup, or freeze for later use as cooking stock.

————— VARIATIONS —————

Caraway seeds, tiny dumplings, fresh green parsley leaves and soft-boiled quails' eggs.

Sliced fresh leek shreds, some crumbled dried morel mushrooms, broken spaghetti pieces and a little chervil.

A handful of watercress, (or landcress), some Jerusalem artichokes, thinly sliced, cubed potato and some saffron threads would impart considerable colour and interest.

Almost-Instant Vegetable Stock

THIS IS an excellent, all-purpose cooking stock with a clearish golden-orange tint. It is also pleasant enough to be used as a clear soup, if one or two lively additions are made or if some more of the original ingredients (but raw) are tossed in, chopped finely, at serving time. It is quick because the vegetables are already finely ground before cooking begins and this makes the slow process of dissolving out the goodness from the foods into the water easy. (This can be applied to any stock and soup-making, by the way, to hasten the taste-producing process. This principle does not apply when making highly starch-laden soups, e.g. potato, or rice, because you are likely to end up with sediment and glue!).

This stock freezes well and can be refrigerated, though like most foods made with fresh ingredients it tastes most lively when newly made. Use this in place of stock cubes and notice the difference!

————— MAKES 1.1 litres (2 pints) —————

2 tomatoes, chopped
1 medium potato, scrubbed and cubed
2 carrots, scrubbed and chopped
4 celery sticks, broken or chopped
2 onions, skinned and chopped
2 cloves garlic, skinned and chopped

1 handful of parsley, stems and leaves,
  coarsely chopped
20 peppercorns
1 cinnamon stick, broken
1.1 litres (2 pints) water
5–7.5 ml (1–1½ level tsp) rock or sea salt

Put the vegetables and garlic into a food processor. Chop well.

Transfer the 6 vegetables to a large soup pan, lidded flameproof pan or casserole, with the parsley, peppercorns and cinnamon stick. Add the measured volume of boiling water. Cover and cook at a rolling simmer for 12–15 minutes.

Strain the stock, pressing out the liquids thoroughly. Taste, add salt as required. Use immediately as stock or soup, or freeze or refrigerate for later use as cooking stock.

————— VARIATIONS —————

Shredded celeriac and/or asparagus shavings (if available), fresh dill and some yellow or green courgette slices or cubes.

A handful of quick-cooking macaroni or tiny pasta stars, some broccoli florets and some dried ceps, crumbled small, and chopped parsley.

Coarse Meaux mustard, single cream, crescents of carrot and cucumber, fresh chives and tiny dumplings.

ASIAN-PACIFIC SOUP STOCK

THIS DEEP mahogany-toned stock is excellent as a soup (with various additions, see below) and as a base for Mongolian Fire Pot Soup (page 52). Fresh ginger is essential. If lemon grass is not available then use dried lemon grass shavings or powder. 2–3 teaspoons of these instead, depending upon pungency. Galangal (or Laos Root), is sometimes known also as lesser galangal. Soya bean paste (Miso) comes ready made in plastic sachets from Japanese vegetarian shops. Lime leaves are wonderfully pungent—these are most easily found in Thai and Indonesian supermarkets. Rice vinegar can be replaced by other vinegar. Almost all of these products will keep, well sealed, in a cool dark place (preferably a refrigerator) for weeks or even months, for use in many recipes. Good fresh garlic (no green central part—if it is present then remove it), and good quality soy are also essentials for good flavours.

MAKES 900 ml (1½ pints)

SERVES 4

2.5 cm (1 inch) length fresh ginger root, grated
2 garlic cloves, peeled and crushed
1 head (or bulb) of lemon grass, quartered lengthways
2.5 cm (1 inch) length fresh laos root (galangal) (optional)
15 g (½ oz) miso (soya bean paste)
2 lime leaves, crushed (optional)
4 celery stalks, broken or chopped

75 g (3 oz) bunch spring onions, chopped (tops reserved)
125 g (4 oz) sweet potato or yam, scrubbed and cubed
1 fresh chilli, whole, slightly crushed
1.1 litres (2 pints) water
15–30 ml (1–2 tbsp) rice, or white wine, vinegar
5–10 ml (1–2 tsp) soy sauce

Put all the ingredients except the vinegar and soy sauce into a large soup pan, flameproof lidded pan, casserole or wok with the water.

Bring to the boil (about 10 minutes), reduce heat to simmer, cover and leave to cook for another 30 minutes. Add the rice wine vinegar and soy sauce and taste. Adjust seasonings.

Strain, pressing out the liquids thoroughly. (Retain the lemon grass for further use if wished.) Add the green tops of the spring onions, chopped. Use immediately as stock or soup, or freeze or refrigerate for later use as cooking stock.

——— VARIATIONS ———

A handful of fine Chinese noodles, some long (or French) beans cut into lengths, some bean curd slivers and a pinch of black beans and some bean sprouts.

Some rehydrated black fungus, sliced baby sweetcorn cobs, sliced into 'coins', rice and shallots, sliced, with a handful of coriander leaves, would taste good also.

Won ton dumplings with ginger and egg filling, sliced bamboo shoots and mustard greens would be lively additions.

MAINSTAY SOUPS

WINTER POND SOUP

MY HUSBAND, Ian, remarked to me that this soup, though tasty, rather resembled a winter's pond, because of its strange garnet-dark colour (given by the dark-gilled mushrooms and the tomato purée) and the half submerged cabbage. It is basic, quick, and not difficult to make. For childish pleasure, you can, if you like, serve it with some 'rafts' of buttered white bread to float on top. This is a warming, sustaining, comforting dish for a winter meal. Dress it up by serving some robust red wine with it, for a more casual meal, drink some good strong beer or cider.

———— MAKES 1.7 litres (3 pints) ————

30 ml (2 tbsp) olive (or other) oil
1 large onion, skinned, halved and sliced
2 Jerusalem artichokes, scrubbed and thinly sliced
6–8 outer leaves of cabbage, rolled and finely shredded
4–6 'flat' or 'open' mushrooms, cut into 1 cm ($\frac{1}{2}$ inch) strips

50 g (2 oz) long grain, arborio or short-grain rice
45 ml (3 level tbsp) tomato purée
7.5–10 ml (1$\frac{1}{2}$–2 level tsp) sea salt
5 ml (1 level tsp) green or black peppercorns
2 or 3 fresh bay leaves, crushed
1 litre (1$\frac{3}{4}$ pints) water

In a non-metal soup pan, sauté the onion and artichoke in the olive oil until aromatic, about 5 minutes.

Add the remaining ingredients, bring to simmering point. Cover, reduce heat, cook for a further 30 minutes. Taste, adjust seasoning if needed.

*S*erve *with bread and butter, rusks or matzoh crackers, for an altogether homely effect.*

MAURICE'S GIROUDET ONION SOUP

THE MAKING of soup with love, attention and skill is an art I hope will never be threatened nor diminished. This soup is simple, yet should not be undertaken carelessly: each distinct aspect contributes to its charm. Such soup was often made for us in an old house in the flat, still landscapes of Eure et Loir, near Chartres, in autumn, winter and early spring evenings, after we'd lunched heartily and felt we needed some clean uncomplicated tastes. It is remarkably substantial, and guaranteed to soothe and renew. This is by no means a classic soup, but it possesses one man's defined style, and recalls happy days.

——— SERVES 4 ———

50 g (2 oz) lightly salted butter
15 ml (1 tbsp) arachide oil
5 large, mild Spanish onions, skinned,
  sliced into rings
sea salt

freshly ground black pepper
1 litre (1¾ pints) boiling water
4 slices stale French bread
50 g (2 oz) Gruyère cheese
dash of cognac or brandy (optional)

In a large frying pan, (or other similar pan) heat the butter and oil until very hot, then toss in all the onions and fry over fierce heat, stirring constantly to coat all the onions until there is a strong aromatic, sweet smell of browning. (The onions must not scorch but neither should they 'stew' up at this stage.)

Reduce heat, cover the pan and leave the onions to soften for 20–30 minutes or thereabouts. (They should become a deep golden colour and almost a pulp.)

Remove the cover, season and pour in about 300 ml (½ pint) of boiling water, stirring the sediment from base of pan. Divide the mixture evenly between 4 large, heatproof, ovenware bowls or dishes. Top up with the remaining boiling water, add extra black pepper to taste. Place bowls in an oven at 200°C/400°F/Gas Mark 6 for about 10 minutes, or until bowls and soup are very hot.

Grate the cheese and cover the bread slices with it. Drop one in each bowl, cheese side upwards, on top of the soup. Leave for 5 minutes longer. If wished, add a dash of cognac to each serving at the table.

*S*erve with some red wine such as a delightful St Amour.

SOUPE MANGE-CLOUD

(Illustrated facing page 32)

LAROUSSE DEFINES Potage Saint-Cloud as a fresh pea purée (Saint Germain) served with diced croûtons fried in butter. Fresh peas are wondrous, though rarely available, and frozen ones too much used, alas. Mange-tout peas should be thought about, too, as a soup ingredient—their tender sweetness is worth exploiting. The *real* charm of my soup lies in the egg-white 'clouds' which float on top to give a witty significance to the name.

——— SERVES 4 ———

25 g (1 oz) butter
30 ml (2 tbsp) extra virgin olive oil
225 g (8 oz) mange-tout peas, stems
   removed, finely sliced
225 g (8 oz) or 1 large onion, sliced
225 g (8 oz) potatoes, scrubbed and cut
   into 6 mm ($\frac{1}{4}$ inch) cubes
50 g (2 oz) Jerusalem artichoke, scrubbed,
   quartered, and finely sliced
750 ml (1$\frac{1}{4}$ pints) vegetable stock

freshly ground sea salt and white pepper
45 ml (3 tbsp) vermouth bianco (sweet
   white vermouth, optional)
150 ml ($\frac{1}{4}$ pint) single cream
2 size 2 egg yolks

CLOUDS:
2 size 2 egg whites
15 ml (1 level tbsp) caster sugar
chopped chives

49

Heat the butter and oil in an attractive, large, heavy, flameproof pan. Add the peas and onion. Toss, stirring over fierce heat until peas are bright green and very glossy and the onion is wilted and translucent (but not browned). Put the pea and onion mixture into a food processor and process, while still hot.

Add the cubed potatoes, artichokes and stock to the pan, bring to boiling, cover, reduce heat and simmer until the potato and artichoke are soft enough to mash with a wooden spoon. Return the pea-purée to the soup, and cook a further 10 minutes.

Pour the soup into the processor. Process only until fairly creamy. Return the soup to the pan. Taste, add seasonings and vermouth, if liked. Reduce heat to gentle simmer.

Whisk the yolks into the cream and pour into the hot soup, stirring well. Turn off heat but leave covered.

Prepare some salted water at simmering point in a large shallow pan, Whisk the egg whites until soft peaks form. Add sugar, whisk again. Spoon 12 portions into the water, and cook for $\frac{1}{2}$–1 minute until the frothy 'clouds' have barely set, then scatter over the chives. Drain and spoon the fluffy 'clouds' on top of the soup, without delay and take soup pan and 'clouds' to the table to serve. (Alternatively, transfer the soup to another, heated serving tureen or separate soup dishes. Drain, put the little 'clouds' in position, and take to table.)

A chilled, fruity-sharp Sauvignon wine could be delightful with this soup, which might have been preceded by either a rice (or cracked wheat) dish of some kind, or a leafy salad (white wine dressing). Good French bread would flatter such a gentle soup, and to follow it might come some fine blue or herbed cheese.

PESTLE SOUP FROM PROVENCE

THOUGH MANY people have heard of pesto and of minestrone, not many are aware that Soupe au Pistou (pistou means pestle) is a substantial 'minestra' type soup/stew, (almost solid with vegetables) served with a pounded paste of fresh basil leaves, garlic, parmesan and olive oil stirred in. Jars of ready made sterilized pesto are a travesty and such watery green sauce (no matter what the provenance) will be sad indeed: never touch this culinary masterpiece unless the pesto is fresh-made. Fresh leaves and other fresh classic ingredients are essential. Fresh pesto or pistou is joyful stuff: to eat, to make, to smell. Traditionally, the white haricot beans are fresh and softish—not long out of their pods. Since these are, in this country, rarely found, 125 g (4 oz) of dried haricots can be used instead.

——— SERVES 4–8 ———

225 g (8 oz) fresh white haricot beans (or pre-soaked dried beans, see above)
2.3 litres (4 pints) water, or fresh vegetable stock
225 g (8 oz) potatoes, scrubbed and cubed
225 g (8 oz) tomatoes, cut into eighths
225 g (8 oz) or 2 leeks, sliced into 1 cm ($\frac{1}{2}$ inch) lengths
225 g (8 oz) orange-fleshed pumpkin, skinned, seeded and cubed
15 ml (1 level tbsp) sea or rock salt crystals
225 g (8 oz) tender young courgettes, diced or chopped
50 g (2 oz) haricot verts (French beans) topped, cut in half
50 g (2 oz) macaroni, broken into pieces

PESTLE SAUCE:
10 ml (2 level tsp) coarse sea or rock salt crystals
5–10 ml (1–2 level tsp) black peppercorns
3–4 garlic cloves, skinned and halved
10–12 fresh basil leaves
125 g (4 oz) freshly grated Parmesan cheese
60–75 ml (2–3 fl oz) pure virgin olive oil
few drops of fresh lemon juice, grappa or cognac (optional)

Put the beans with the water or stock in a large, lidded flameproof soup pan or casserole. Bring up to boiling, reduce the heat, part-cover and simmer for 30 minutes.

Add the potatoes, tomatoes, leeks and pumpkin and cook for a further 40 minutes until the vegetables are meltingly tender.

Add the courgettes, trimmed green beans, and broken lengths of macaroni or spaghetti. Cover and cook for a further 25 minutes.

Make the Pestle Sauce. Using a pestle and mortar, pound the salt, pepper, garlic and some of the basil, first gently, then more forcibly, to a paste. Add the remaining leaves, (roughly torn just before addition) and increase pressure to obtain a brilliant green purée. Add some of the cheese, continue pounding, add some of the oil, to loosen the texture somewhat. Continue this process until all the ingredients are used up. Add a dash of lemon, grappa or cognac if wished (but this is hardly traditional).

By now the vegetables should be cooked to perfection, the broth flavourful and the pasta plump, swollen and soft.

Serve the soup in its pan at the table with a ladle. Diners spoon some of the purée into their soup bowls as they are served.

RED LENTIL POTTAGE

THE FOOD value of lentils is high and their use goes far back into antiquity. Red, so-called Egyptian, lentils have often had less culinary cachet than the whole, larger, olive green and brown European varieties, though all lentils can be coaxed into deliciousness without much effort, and a little imagination. Lentils are better not soaked, but need careful sorting to remove stones and occasional mud, though a good supplier will save considerable time and work on your part. This colourful soup is lively, nourishing and inexpensive. It is pleasant eaten cold as a dip.

——— SERVES 4 ———

125 g (4 oz) red lentils
5 ml (1 tsp) fruity olive oil
1.1 litres (2 pints) vegetable stock or water
bouquet of fresh herbs including bay leaves, crushed, and thyme sprigs
125 g (4 oz) onion, skinned and chopped
10 ml (2 level tsp) coriander seeds, crushed
10 ml (2 level tsp) dill seeds, crushed
30 ml (2 level tbsp) tomato purée (or harissa)

1 small, dried, seeded red chilli pepper, crumbled
5 ml (1 level tsp) sweet paprika
225 g (8 oz) carrots, scrubbed and finely sliced
225 g (8 oz) celery sticks, sliced diagonally
30 ml (2 tbsp) fruit vinegar or balsamic vinegar
salt
freshly ground pepper
5–10 ml (1–2 level tsp) parsley, freshly chopped

Clean the lentils, discarding any foreign bodies. Heat the olive oil in a heavy-based pan and fry the lentils for a few minutes, to develop their flavour. Add the stock or water and bay leaves and thyme, bring to the boil, cover and reduce heat to simmering. Cook for 20 minutes or until tender.

Add the onion, coriander and dill seeds. Stir in the purée (tomato gives a milder, fruity flavour, harissa a spicier, hotter flavour), the chilli and the paprika, and the finely sliced carrot and celery. Stir well to blend.

Simmer, uncovered for a further 40 minutes. Remove the bay leaf, taste, add vinegar and adjust seasonings. Serve as it is or puréed in a food processor or blender. Serve scattered with parsley.

51

MONGOLIAN FIRE POT SOUP

(Illustrated facing page 65)

MONGOLIAN HOT POT, or Imperial Fire Pot (*Sha Jang Joo*) traditionally includes meats (cut wafer thin), often bean curd and vegetables, noodles and dried mushrooms, cooked at the table in a vessel which contains a central chimney with live coals. The broth becomes more and more tasty as each item of food is cooked or re-heated in it before being dipped in aromatics and eaten. The soup is drunk last.

My version contains no meat or fish but a selection of tasty and bland foods. It is wonderful for entertaining. Issue each guest with chopsticks or a wire or bamboo scoop, their share of 'dunking' foods nearby, as well as some communal soy sauce, seasoned salt, seasoned pepper, a fruit sauce (hoi sin for example) and raw egg yolks for those who like them (the hot food is coated by the egg, which sets on contact). A ladle will be required at the end. (Use a flameproof pot with candle if the authentic vessel is unavailable. If you do use a real fire pot, make sure the hot vessel with its burning charcoal stands upon a heatproof tile, marble slab, stone or tray to prevent the table from becoming scorched.)

——— SERVES 4 ———

1.7 litres (3 pints) Asian-Pacific Soup Stock (see page 46) or vegetable stock (containing soy, garlic, ginger, chilli)
3–4 lime leaves (optional)
spring onions, chopped
For cooking in the stock: (to be divided into quarters, one for each diner)
50 g (2 oz) dried wooden ear mushrooms, (re-hydrated in boiling water for 20 minutes) sliced, or fresh shiitake mushrooms
50 g (2 oz) dried black fungus (re-hydrated in hot water for 20 minutes)
125 g (4 oz) tofu (silken soy bean curd) cut into 8 or 12 blocks
125 g (4 oz) mange-tout peas, topped

125 g (4 oz) choy sum (Chinese yellow flowering mustard greens, type)
125 g (4 oz) water chestnuts or bamboo shoots, skinned and sliced
225 g (8 oz) baby sweetcorn on the cob
225 g (8 oz) quick-cooking Chinese egg noodles of your choice
25 g (1 oz) Chinese preserved vegetables, finely sliced (optional)

DIPS:
Seed, Nut and Herb Citrus Seasoning (see page 37)
Polyglot Hot Seasoning (page 38)
Seaweed Greens Seasoning (page 39)
Soy Sauce, fruit sauce, egg yolks (2 or 3) (optional)

Heat the soup and add to the cooking pot, which has already been lit. Add the lime leaves, if wished, and the spring onions. Cover the pan at intervals to prevent undue evaporation.

Encourage diners to deposit, then scoop or lift out each piece of food and touch it into the seasoning or seasonings of their choice. Try to finish with the noodles though there is invariably some pleasant confusion about the whole procedure—part of the fun.

Ladle soup and noodles into the bowl of each diner towards the end, and add fragments of Chinese preserved vegetables, if wished.

Complete the Chinese banquet theme by finishing with some carved tropical fruits in an arrangement: mango diamonds, pawpaw segments, half-peeled lichees and some Chinese pears, perhaps, then some sweetened rice cakes or sweetmeats or some steamed buns. Pass scented hot towels and have some warm yellow wine (Shaohsing), or Fukien, or Keemun tea if preferred, with the meal.

Exotic foods such as lime leaves, shiitake and black fungus, tofu, noodles, choy sum and even fresh, black skinned water chestnuts are often available from Oriental and other major supermarkets. While Thai and Japanese specialty stores will also probably stock fire pots, scoops, ladles and so on.

SOUPE CHAUMIERE

THE WORD *chaumière* conjures up a country cottage feeling, something homely. This soup is, however, just as much a high-rise city dweller's supper—smooth, simple and made from ordinary fresh ingredients: all you need is a decent greengrocer. Chervil can grow in window boxes if you are green fingered; if you are not, then young flat leaf parsley is a boon. A handful can mean 5 or 15 grams—it's up to you: this measure is precise in its deliberate imprecision!

——— SERVES 4 ———

53

2 large leeks, white parts only
350 g (12 oz) tomatoes, or 1 large
*   marmande tomato*
350 g (12 oz) old potatoes, scrubbed clean
225 g (8 oz) cauliflower florets
50 g (2 oz) butter
2 sugar lumps, crushed

5 ml (1 level tsp) sea salt
600 ml (1 pint) boiling water or stock
thick cream or thick yogurt
freshly ground black pepper
handful of fresh chervil or young, flat leaf
*   parsley*

Slice the leeks finely crossways, wash well and drain. Dice the tomatoes (skin, flesh and seeds).

Heat and melt the butter in a heavy, flameproof, lidded casserole. Add the leeks and soften them, stirring frequently, without allowing them to brown. Add the tomatoes and allow to cook for 5 minutes or until they soften and begin to become pulpy. Dice and add the potatoes. Divide the cauliflower into tiny florets and add. Stir in the crushed sugar lumps, the salt and the liquid and bring back to boiling point.

Reduce the heat, cover and simmer for 15 minutes, then put the contents of the pan into a food processor or blender and reduce to a smooth purée, in short bursts. Return to the pan and bring back to near boiling. Reduce heat.

Stir in the cream or yogurt. Check the taste, add pepper. Serve with freshly torn sprigs of chervil on top, or roughly chopped parsley.

COOL, CLEAR AND FRUITED SOUPS

TRIANGLE SOUP

ALL THIS soup contains are 3, perfectly united, but elementary ingredients: fresh, meltingly-ripe and fragrant pears, ginger ale and fresh raspberries. Nothing is cooked, and the whole thing takes less than 10 minutes to make. Set in glass dishes over ice, this comes to the table a triumph of simplicity, good indeed. It is refreshing as a start to a winter meal, and is perfect as a late summer offering as well. Sometimes I have been almost tempted to add a wisp of crème fraîche, a trail of yogurt, a spoonful of low fat yogurt, even a sprinkle of mixed spice. But I always resist. It is better left alone. What *is* essential is to have those perfect, bite-sized portions of pear and some whole berries in the soup itself. Serve with some scented white wine—golden Sauternes, Monbazillac, sweetish Vouvray or a Moscato—and lacy tuiles biscuits.

—————— SERVES 4 ——————

700 g (1½ lb) ripe, scented dessert pears
600 ml (1 pint) dry ginger ale

450 g (1 lb) fresh raspberries

Check the pears. Although firm, they should 'give' a little at the neck, yet be juicy enough to trickle when bitten into. Peel them, halve, quarter and core them. Cross-cut each quarter. Put one half pear, prepared, into each soup bowl. Scatter 225 g (8 oz) of the raspberries over the pears (as if on a raft).

Put the remaining pears and berries and a quarter of the ginger ale into a blender or food processor. (Use a juicer, if one is available, for the fruits, then add the ginger ale to this.) Blend, in short bursts, until a smooth purée is achieved. Dilute with remaining liquid. Process again, briefly. Pour the soup over the fruits gently. Serve without too much delay if possible (although this is a good-natured soup, and can tolerate being made in advance).

For an excellent brunch, lunch or late supper a good selection of cheeses with crisp fresh celery, (or a cheese-based pastry or cheesy pasta of some kind), good crusty brown bread and some walnuts, could follow this soup. Good coffee would be welcome, too.

54

DORIS-ROSA JELLIED SOUP

(Illustrated facing page 32)

I WAS NEWLY married and newly arrived from the south. We had come to live in one of New Zealand's best orchard areas, Hawkes Bay. I kept noticing sign boards beside the road simply stating the 2 words: BLACK DORIS. This sounded fearsome and fascinating; a Maori warning, a lost tribe? Black Doris turned out to be a deep red, fleshy, scented plum, utterly captivating. Santa Rosa plums are similarly aromatic, voluptuous and juicy. Try to select superb dark plums for this slightly jellied soup— (helped by a little tapioca—every schoolboy's dread), and serve it in small soup cups icy cold, with a bowl of soured cream or yogurt nearby if wished. This makes a bright prelude to a meal—one's taste buds start jumping!

MAKES 4 SMALL SERVINGS

*350 g (12 oz) dark red fleshed, aromatic
  plums
1 cinnamon stick, whole
300 ml (½ pint) water
20 ml (4 level tsp) 'seed pearl' tapioca
50 g (2 oz) caster sugar
1 small lemon, freshly shredded zest and
  juice*

*TO SERVE:
30 ml (2 tbsp) mirabelle, quetsch, slivovitz
  or other plum eau de vie or fruit brandy
  (optional)
4 or 8 fresh mint leaves*

55

Slice the flesh from the fruits in eighths into a non-metal pan, discarding the stones.

Add the cinnamon stick and water. Bring to simmering, cover and cook for 15–20 minutes or until pulpy. Remove the cinnamon stick.

Sprinkle the tapioca over the fruit, stir in quickly, reduce the heat and add the sugar. Leave to cook for a further 6–8 minutes until bubbling and thick. The tapioca should turn completely translucent.

If wished, purée the soup briefly in a blender or food processor, or else leave as it is. Add lemon zest and juice. Chill quickly over ice or in the freezer if wished, for 8–10 minutes, then leave to chill and 'jell' slightly for 2–3 hours (if the mixture looks too firm, thin with a little water or white wine).

*Just before serving, stir the liquor (if used) through the ruby-red
soup. Serve in soup cups, decorated with mint leaves.*

GUAVA, BANANA AND ACACIA SOUP

JELLY-LIKE fruity soups need some special quality, in my opinion, to justify their use at the start of a meal, rather than as a dessert. Guavas, scented wonderfully, are worthy of such treatment. Serve this soup chilled, in cups, with hot and lacy melba toasts (or even cinnamon toasts), used as the 'taste-tempters' to begin a lively meal. No extra setting agent is added: the pectin of the fruits gives a thick and jelly-like texture. Be adventurous with your choice of citrus fruits: there are many, now, on the market to choose from.

——— MAKES 4–6 SERVINGS ———

2 or 3 ripe (barely soft, but scented) fresh
  green-gold guavas
2 bananas (firm, barely soft)
2 clementines, tangerines, mandarines or
  Temple oranges, zest and freshly
  squeezed juice

450 ml (¾ pint) dry sparkling cider
30 ml (2 level tbsp) acacia honey

TO SERVE:
acacia flowers or other decorative blooms
  (optional decoration)

Use a peeler to thinly remove skin from guavas (if this is impossible it means the fruit are too ripe for this recipe). Halve then crosscut the fruit (and seeds) into 1 cm (½ inch) slices, and put into a small pan with the peeled bananas sliced in a similar manner. Add the juice from the citrus fruits. Reserve the zest.

Add just enough cider to half cover the fruit, cover and simmer for 10 minutes or until very aromatic. The fruit should be able to be crushed using a fork.

Purée the fruit with half the remaining cider in a blender or food processor. Sieve, using a plastic or stainless steel sieve (seeds may cause broken teeth!). Stir in remaining cider, chill quickly over ice or in the freezer (about 8–10 minutes). Leave in the refrigerator to chill and 'jell' slightly, for a few hours, or overnight. Serve in small soup cups, each with 1 or 2 ice cubes on top plus the reserved zest, and an acacia flower tucked into the napkin or beside each of the soup cups.

Ordinary metal sieves may give a metallic taste because of the acidity of the fruit reacting with the metal: try to use a non-metal sieve, or a stainless steel sieve.

56

EFFIE'S GREEN SPRING SOUP

(Illustrated facing page 32)

AN ACQUAINTANCE who is both a gourmet and an enthusiastic, accomplished cook gave me the idea for this singular soup. Her version uses no watercress and more spinach, and 'when particularly in need of vitamins' she adds even more parsley—a positive attitude which I applaud, in springtime or indeed any other time. Chill it quickly, over ice, or make it 4 or 5 hours ahead, so it is very cold indeed, doubly refreshing. Vary the consistency as wished.

Issue each diner with half a lemon or lime. Juice should be squeezed into each spoonful as it is eaten, for an absolute celebration of flavours.

——— SERVES 4–6 ———

50 g (2 oz) spinach or spinach beet
200 g (7 oz), or 1 large bunch, fresh coriander
100 g (4 oz) bunch flat leaf parsley
275 g (10 oz) watercress
900 ml (1½ pints) vegetable stock
225 g (8 oz) potatoes
sea salt and freshly ground black pepper
bay leaf

2.5 cm (1 inch) length of fresh root ginger, peeled and chopped
3 cloves garlic, skinned and chopped
5 ml (1 level tsp) whole cumin seeds
4 whole green cardamom pods
10 ml (2 level tsp) nigella seeds (optional)
150–300 ml (¼–½ pint) buttermilk or natural yogurt
2 fresh limes or lemons, halved

Check that the spinach, coriander, parsley and cress are perfectly clean, then chop them coarsely, leaves, stems and all. Put into a food processor or blender and process in 3 or 4 batches, using brief bursts, to give a rich green mixture.

Bring the stock to the boil and add the finely cubed potatoes, the sea salt, pepper and bay leaf. Bring to the boil again, cover the pan and simmer for 8–10 minutes or until the potato is tender.

Put the garlic, ginger, cumin seeds, and cardamon seeds (in their pods), and nigella seeds, if liked, into the goblet of an electric coffee grinder or mortar. Grind or pound until crushed and aromatic.

Remove the bay leaf from the potatoes, then pour the contents of the pan into the food processor or blender and process to a coarse purée. Return the purée to the pan adding the herbs and spice mixture. Bring almost to boiling (about 5 minutes) then add the desired amount of buttermilk or yogurt and simmer for a further few minutes until heated, and flavours have blended. Cool quickly over ice. Allow to grow cold.

Traditionalists will enjoy Melba toast and icy cold butter curls as additional complements, and I have found that chilled Aquavit, clean and brisk, is an unusual but good accompaniment, served freezing cold in tiny, iced glasses.

PLANTAIN AND PEANUT SOUP MARTINIQUE

ICED FRUIT and nut soups are unusual, but the combination of tastes is interesting and the dishes themselves are thoroughly nutritious. Plantains are often found in ethnic markets and Afro-Caribbean stores. They look like large odd-coloured bananas—they must be cooked before being eaten. In this recipe they are baked. Make sure you follow the instructions—they are baked in their skins and then peeled, rather than the other way around. Plantains have a good flavour and are an interesting vegetable.

———— SERVES 4 ————

2 firm (not hard) dark-skinned plantains
125 g (4 oz) shelled, roasted and salted
   peanuts, roughly chopped
1.1 litres (2 pints) homemade vegetable
   stock or water
2.5 ml (½ level tsp) salt
freshly ground pepper

5 ml (1 tsp) Angostura bitters
5–10 ml (1–2 tsp) chilli or Tabasco sauce
thin cream (as required)
60 ml (4 tbsp) dark rum
edible flower petals
2 limes or 2 small lemons (optional)

Slice the plantains lengthways into 4 'boats'. Bake, cut surfaces uppermost, at 200°C/400°F/Gas Mark 6 for 18–20 minutes, or until the flesh is tender and aromatic, yellowed and firm. Remove and discard the skin, chop the plantain flesh.

Put the peanuts, a portion at a time, with some stock into a blender or food processor and blend to a paste. Repeat the process until all remaining peanuts are used, but not all of the stock.

Put the plantain flesh into the blender with some stock and blend until smooth. Return this with remaining purée to a large saucepan.

Bring to a gentle boil, reduce heat and simmer, covered, for 10–12 minutes. Add salt, pepper, bitters and chilli sauce and heat through. Taste and adjust seasonings. Cool over ice.

Stir in some cream and the rum at serving time. Scatter some edible flower petals over. Serve in bowls set over ice and pass each diner a decoratively cut lime or lemon half to squeeze into their soup as they eat.

Serve chilled lager or medium dry white wine with this soup and follow with a rice dish of some kind (perhaps a hot risotto) and a crisp salad. A cheese pastry or savoury and fresh tropical fruit could finish off this meal.

58

MELON, CARROT AND TOMATO SOUP

(Illustrated facing page 32)

DIFFERENCES IN temperature within the one dish can be intriguing and refreshing. This hot soup is served in icy cold melon 'cups', with icy melon cubes acting as a balance to the other colours and textures. It can be expensive to make, however, for it requires 3 small, scented, ogen melons. Make this soup when they are at their best and cheapest. Either baby or matronly carrots work equally well in this recipe and ready made passato (tomato pulp) is useful and suitable in this soup, which has been described as having 'angel-hair' texture, because of the carrot shreds. It is a pretty pink colour.

———— SERVES 4 ————

3 ripe, scented ogen melons
225 g (8 oz) medium or small carrots
2 shallots, skinned
150 ml ($\frac{1}{4}$ pint) vegetable stock or water
150 ml ($\frac{1}{4}$ pint) tomato juice, passato or
  freshly juiced tomatoes

125 ml (4 fl oz) Niersteiner or similar
  sweet wine
2.5–5 ml ($\frac{1}{2}$–1 tsp) Angostura bitters
salt to taste
French bread

Halve the 3 melons crossways and discard the seeds and membranes. Chill. Scoop the flesh from 2 of the melon halves. Cube or 'ball' the flesh and put aside to chill.

Using a food processor (shredder attachment) grate or shred the carrots and shallots, and put into a non-metal soup pan with the vegetable stock or water, tomato juice and wine. Add half the melon. Bring gently to boiling, reduce heat and simmer for 5 minutes.

Reduce to a purée in a food processor or blender, adding bitters once the soup is blended.

Pour some soup into each melon 'cup', drop several icy melon chunks on top and serve. Encourage the diners to scrape some cold melon from the inner walls of each melon half while enjoying the hot soup. Serve with French bread.

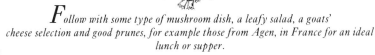

*F*ollow *with some type of mushroom dish, a leafy salad, a goats'*
cheese selection and good prunes, for example those from Agen, in France for an ideal
lunch or supper.

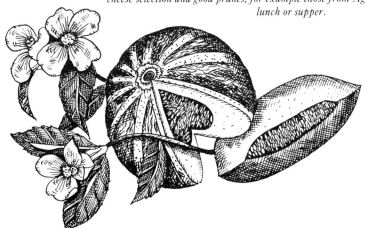

59

PUZZLE SOUP DIP

FOR ME, unusual combinations of natural textures, tastes, colours and aromas can be puzzling but fun. Inventing new recipes is, after all, a sort of culinary alchemy! This concoction is delicate, delicious and yet oddly tan-coloured. It is simple yet successful. Make it in 10 minutes to use fairly promptly. It can also be almost considered a dip.

––––– SERVES 4 OR 6 –––––

3 medium or 2 large, ripe avocados
150 ml ($\frac{1}{4}$ pint) orange juice, freshly
    squeezed
150 ml ($\frac{1}{4}$ pint) natural low fat yogurt
    ice-cold
5 ml (1 tsp) citrus flower water
150 ml ($\frac{1}{4}$ pint) iced mineral water, (or
    50/50 hock and water)

175–225 g (6–8 oz) fresh blueberries
2.5 ml ($\frac{1}{2}$ level tsp) salt

TO SERVE:
langues de chat biscuits, saffron brioche (see
    page 35, Zaffymec Horseshoe Brioche),
    or other bread

Skin and stone the avocado; cube the flesh. Put into a bowl with the orange juice and yogurt. Process, or blend, to a purée. Stir in the citrus flower water and enough water, (or hock and water), to give a pleasing soup consistency.

Pour into soup bowls or large soup cups. Decorate each with a handful of berries so that they float on top.

Because this is quite a rich soup, all that may be needed after it may be a potato, pasta or rice salad then some strong cheese, (perhaps Livarot or Coulommiers) and some nuts and dried fruit, perhaps.

The Central Course

VERY MAIN meal demands its centrepiece, its set piece, its *pièce de resistance*. Here, in this chapter, is embodied much of the mainstream of the book: those sustaining, well balanced, interesting but in the end comforting dishes which allow us to leave the table knowing 'I have dined today'.

I have decided to group the recipes into what I find to be the subject-basis of the dishes. Some are mushroom-based (and a wide range are covered), some egg-centred (but never in isolation—the egg combines with vegetables, fruit, within crumbles, pastries or sauces), yet others are cheese-inspired or centred around a specific fresh vegetable or grain or pulse—even the humble potato has style!

Homemade pasta features in this chapter. Ever since I borrowed a pasta machine 3 years ago and began to experiment with fresh pasta which could be made, cooked and eaten *within 15 minutes,* I have longed to include a few of my best findings in a book. Here they are. If you have never dared, or dared and failed, to make your own pasta, do try these recipes (they may seem long but this is in order to make it easy for you). No guesswork is involved, even for beginners. It is a near-magical experience to loop long skeins of rainbow colours from one's pasta machine—like an alchemist's loom!

In many instances, for the true food enthusiast, the ideal way to round off a proper meal is with some splendid cheeses, then a helping of simple, beautiful fresh fruits. To me this European inspired pattern of eating is a wonderful way to balance many meals, and it is both healthful and practical. It also reflects the changing of the seasons. Oriental, Middle Eastern or African-style main dishes may require a different approach.

I always think of the whole meal, so in addition to recipe instructions, I have provided lively guidelines (but never directives) about which drinks to choose to accompany this or that main course, what particular salad, bread, dressing or accompaniment might also be relevant, and what preceding and following courses might be used within the context of the particular meal. The introduction and the additional notes I have provided with each recipe are therefore more important here than in most cookery books.

EGG AND CHEESE CHOICES

POTTED BROCCOLI WITH STILTON

THIS SUBSTANTIAL cold vegetable dish is easy, decorative and delicious—it needs plain, unbuttered lacy-textured bread with it. While the flavours are robust, the nutty delicacy of the broccoli itself is really delicious hidden amongst so many other strong tastes. The vegetables sit neatly in a cheese-marbled dome, on a disc of nut-studded butter, which is eaten with the dish. Because this is both strong flavoured and rich, you need only serve very simple dishes before or after it.

——— SERVES 4 ———

30 ml (2 tbsp) dark sesame oil
450 g (1 lb) broccoli spears, separated into
   tiny florets
225 g (8 oz) creamy Stilton, crumbled
150 ml ($\frac{1}{4}$ pint) fino sherry
10 ml (2 tsp) Worcestershire sauce

1.25 ml ($\frac{1}{4}$ tsp) Tabasco (or other hot
   pepper sauce)
75 g (3 oz) unsalted butter
75 g (3 oz) pecan nuts, shelled
1 loaf crusty French bread

Heat the sesame oil in a wok, frying pan or other large shallow pan. Add the broccoli florets all at once and toss over fierce heat for 3–5 minutes until brilliant green and bite-tender (firm but not raw), covering the pan for the last minute or so. Uncover. Leave to stand.

Quickly blend the Stilton and fino and the 2 sauces roughly together using a food processor or blender, or with a fork if the weather is hot and cheese soft. Stir the still-warm broccoli into the cheese mixture until it is fairly evenly distributed. Press into a 1.1 litre (2 pint) deep mould, bowl or curved dish, not more than 12.5 cm (5 inches) across. Level the top. Scatter over the nuts. Melt the unsalted butter gently, then pour over the top of the broccoli, cheese and nuts. Chill until the butter has set and the broccoli has completely cooled (about 1$\frac{1}{2}$–2 hours).

Serve with a lot of lacy bread (or toasted ficelle), additional chilled fino or some really top vintage character port. Barolo would suit those who prefer to drink unfortified wine with this course.

HARRY'S BAR SAFFRONATA WITH PEAS

T HE MOST delicious penne I have ever been served was some I watched being cooked in the kitchens of the famous Harry's Bar in Mayfair. I was to prepare similarly authentic fare to be photographed in a studio miles away the next morning, and the proprietor, James Sherwood, had made it known that the staff must show us what standards to expect. After consultation about the linens, cutlery, serving tools, flowers, lighting and the beauteous blue-rimmed Venetian glass water pitchers (stunning), I watched the chef at work. He cooked with tremendous élan at great speed. Penne had never been a favourite of mine, I found the tubular solidness unsympathetic. He changed my mind. Tucked up, later, at the bar, sticks of wholewheat, hand-made grissini (flown in from Venice) by my side, and a glass of good Venetian red wine in my right hand, I experienced genuine delight at the delicacy of this lovely dish. Here, to the best of my memory, is my version of that feat. The pea garnish is entirely my own, however.

——— SERVES 4 ———

350 g (12 oz) penne (medium sized)
50 g (2 oz) unsalted butter
*2 generous pinches (2 sachets) saffron
    strands (or powdered pure saffron)*
15 ml (1 tbsp) grappa
300 ml ($\frac{1}{2}$ pint) thick cream
150 ml ($\frac{1}{4}$ pint) single cream

freshly ground salt
black pepper
*75 g (3 oz) freshly grated Parmesan or
    Romano cheese*
*125 g (4 oz) fresh mange-tout peas, topped
    and tailed*

Add the penne to a large pan of rapidly boiling salted water—at least 2.3 litres (4 pints). Bring back to boiling and cook, at a lively boil, uncovered, for 10–12 minutes or until 'al dente'—firm enough to retain their shape but not at all hard. Drain the pasta and keep hot. While the pasta cooks, sprinkle the saffron shreds into a heatproof wine glass or cup and add the grappa. Stand in warm water, swirling the two and crushing down occasionally, until a brilliant yellow develops.

Put the butter into a medium, heavy-based pan. Heat until hot and bubbling. Add the saffron-grappa mixture and the creams. Cook rapidly to a bubbling sauce. Heat the grill to very hot.

Empty the penne into the pan, shaking it with a back and forward motion (not stirring) over the heat to coat each pasta tube. Quickly slice the mange-tout (held in bunches of 8 or 10), into 5 diagonal shreds. Scatter these over the top of the penne in their glossy sauce at serving time. Pour on to a heated serving platter, add the cheese and flash the dish beneath a preheated grill to glaze the top.

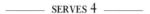

*S erve with good bread sticks and some red or white wine and
follow the dish with a red-leafed salad with croûtons, perhaps, and maybe some
peaches in champagne to follow the (now legendary) Bellini tradition. Fresh figs
would be another alternative.*

63

MOZZARELLA, TOMATO AND SUNFLOWER NOODLES

THIS TWENTY-MINUTE lunch or supper dish is not difficult to achieve as long as you have a sharp serrated knife, an electric kettle and a preheated grill. It is the textural contrasts which make the dish appealing, as well as good simple tastes and colours. I find that Japanese buckwheat soba noodles (available, dried in 225 g (8 oz) packs) have more curious a texture beneath the tongue than ordinary round buckwheat spaghetti. The Japanese noodles are rectangular, cost more, and are somewhat more involved to cook than the spaghetti equivalent. Select the type which suits you better but follow the relevant cooking instructions and timing guides.

——— SERVES 4 ———

3 large, underripe marmande (beefsteak) tomatoes
2 × 175 g (6 oz) mozzarella cheeses
olive oil for greasing
30–45 ml (2–3 level tbsp) plain, or seasoned, sunflower seeds
225 g (8 oz) dried Japanese soba (buckwheat) noodles, or buckwheat spaghetti
15 ml (1 level tbsp) sea salt

DRESSING:
1 garlic clove, skinned and finely chopped
30 ml (2 tbsp) olive oil
15 ml (1 tbsp) fruit vinegar, (e.g. raspberry)
45–60 ml (3–4 level tbsp) chopped fresh parsley

Remove stalks from tomatoes and turn them stalk side downwards. Slice each into 10 slices using a sharp, stainless steel, serrated knife. Slice each mozzarella crossways to give 15 or 16 thin slices, using the same blade, and a sawing motion. Lightly oil a foil-covered baking sheet, or grill pan grid (folding up the foil at the edges into a rim). Alternate tomato and cheese slices in a series of 4 lines, laid overlapping like roof tiles. Scatter over the sunflower seeds.

Put the noodles into the boiling water with the salt and cook until 'al dente'. When the pasta is half-cooked, put the tomato-cheese-seed mixture under the heated grill (about 5 cm (2 inches) beneath) and cook until the tomatoes are heated and juicy and the mozzarella is gently melting (if it overcooks it will trickle and lose its pleasing consistency: if this seems imminent, reduce heat or increase the distance from heat).

Make the dressing by shaking or stirring together the 4 ingredients in a screw-topped jar, or bowl.

Drain the noodles, toss in the dressing, pile on to the serving dish or dishes. Lift quarter-sections of the tomato-cheese-seed mixture, onto the noodles.

LEFT TO RIGHT IN THE GLASSES: LASSITUDE COCKTAIL (PAGE 13), SESAME EGG FROTH (PAGE 15), MIDSUMMER FROTH (PAGE 12) AND IN THE FOREGROUND ZAFFYMEC HORSESHOE BRIOCHE (PAGE 35), LEFT AND EGGS MENAGE A TROIS (PAGE 28), RIGHT

Hot Avocado and Goats' Cheese Sandwiches

THIS IS simple (but lively) luncheon or supper food: scented, buttery crusts are topped with oozing toasted goats' cheese and the melifluous smoothness of warm avocado. A little bed of fresh green leaves beneath each sandwich and a touch of good vinaigrette with herbs completes the picture. Though French cheeses are my favourites, good fresh local goats' cheeses fit the bill perfectly well, if they are reasonably compact in texture.

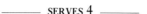

———— SERVES 4 ————

1 cm ($\frac{1}{2}$ inch) thick slices of firm granary, wholewheat or similar bread
20 ml (4 level tsp) soft unsalted butter
1 clove garlic, skinned and crushed
2 × 100 g (4 oz) Chavignol (French) or other firm textured goat cheese
2 large ripe avocados, skinned and stoned
60 ml (4 tbsp) vinaigrette (made with olive oil and white Sancerre or other white wine)
15 ml (1 tbsp) snipped chives, parsley or chervil

TO SERVE:
additional fresh herbs
50 g (2 oz) corn salad (mâche or lamb's lettuce)
25–50 g (1–2 oz) young dandelion or spinach leaves

Preheat a grill to very hot. Toast one side of the 4 slices of bread until golden and crusty. Mix the butter and garlic.

Spread the untoasted surface of the bread with the garlic butter.

Halve the goats' cheeses crossways, or else cut a cheese baton into 4 equal discs. Lay the cheese, cut surfaces upwards, on the bread. Grill for 45–60 seconds. (Keep careful watch that the goats' cheese bubbles but does not overheat, reducing the heat if necessary.)

Slice the halved, stoned avocados crossways into thick crescents.

Pile the sliced avocado around the cheese on each sandwich and return to the grill for a further 15–20 seconds so that the avocado warms through.

Spoon a little vinaigrette over the avocados, place each hot sandwich upon a banquette of mixed green leaves, sprinkling over any remaining dressing.

Eat without delay, accompanied, (if you are lucky enough), with some good crisp Sancerre. Have a black pepper mill at hand.

MONGOLIAN FIRE POT SOUP (PAGE 52) AND IN THE BLUE AND WHITE BOWL
SEED, NUT AND HERB CITRUS SEASONING (PAGE 37) AND ABOVE IT POLYGLOT HOT SEASONING (PAGE 38). ALSO SHOWN
ARE, FROM FRONT TO BACK, CHINESE PEARS, CHINESE NOODLES, EGG YOLKS, SOY SAUCE, CHOY SUM, WATER
CHESTNUTS, TOFU, BABY SWEETCORN, BLACK FUNGUS AND WOOD EAR MUSHROOMS

OJJA TAJINE ZEINEB KAAK (with harissa cream)

TAJINES ARE North African dishes which often take their name from the vessels in which they are cooked (rather as we use the word casserole). *Ojja* means egg in Tunisia. The tajines we tasted on a recent holiday varied from meat, vegetables and egg 'stews' to omelette or custard-like dishes in which many tasty ingredients were set. Depending upon size, shape and surface area and whether they are cooked in china or metal dishes, they will vary in brownness and crustiness. Often the tajines we tasted contained aubergines, sometimes saffron, and sometimes dried marigold petals. My adaptation was aided by a good local publication, 'La Sofra' by Zeineb Kaak, an accomplished cook by all accounts. Boukha is a fig brandy.

———— SERVES 4 ————

450 g (1 lb) fresh spinach, washed
125 g (4 oz) French green beans, topped and tailed and cut crossways in half
25–50 ml (1–2 fl oz) stock or water
sea salt to taste
45 ml (3 tbsp) fruity olive oil
1 medium onion, skinned and chopped
125 g (4 oz) firm, white, sharp-flavoured cheese (such as Feta or Wensleydale), crumbled or cubed

125 g (4 oz) black olives, stones removed
1.25 ml ($\frac{1}{4}$ tsp) saffron strands
15 ml (1 tbsp) Boukha (or other fruit brandy or similar white spirit)
8 medium eggs, beaten

SAUCE:
15–30 ml (1–2 level tbsp) harissa paste
125 ml (4 fl oz) natural yogurt, fromage blanc or fromage frais

Cook the wet spinach in a heavy based pan, covered, until the volume has halved and the colour is a brilliant green. Shake the lidded pan from time to time. The spinach should be bite-tender, about 3–5 minutes should suffice, depending upon age. Drain, pressing out the liquid. Chop the spinach lightly. Cook the beans in the cooking water, adding extra stock or water if needed, so that they are almost covered. Cover the pan and boil for 3–4 minutes or until the beans are brilliant green and bite-tender. Drain, add to the spinach.

Heat the oil in a pan and soften the onion in the oil over moderate heat until it is translucent. Add the crumbled or cubed cheese, the 2 green vegetables and the black olives. Toss all together to mix.

In a separate cup or glass infuse the saffron in the spirit, heating it over a little hot water, and pressing the strands a little to extract the scent and colour.

Whisk the eggs until light and frothy. Put the vegetables, cheese mixture, and saffron liquid into the egg mixture, stir to blend. Turn the tajine mixture into an oiled 900 g (2 lb) loaf tin, standing in a larger baking dish. Bake in an oven at 200°C/400°F/Gas Mark 6 for 30 minutes or until the mixture is firm and golden on top. (Test using a knife blade—it should emerge clean.)

Leave to stand for 2–3 minutes, uncovered, run a knife around the edge to loosen the tajine, then invert on to a heated serving plate in one brisk movement. To make the sauce, blend the harissa with the yogurt, fromage frais or blanc until creamy-smooth.

Serve the tajine with slices already cut and with the sauce poured around it.

66

Potato Gratin with Egg-Lemon Topping

UNDER A pleasantly egg-modified cheese topping (no crumbs, however) lie layers of potato and onion stacked up against the edges of the flameproof dish rather like roof tiles. Herbs and delectable nut oil give great charm. In this recipe the nuts replace crumbs, giving pleasant crunch along with the strong-flavoured cheese. Do use a good, preferably farmhouse type, cheese for this dish, not the packaged 'plastic' variety. Cabrales is a good Spanish cheese, Pecorino an Italian hard variety, or go for farmhouse Cheddar. Talk to your cheese merchant.

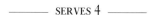

——— SERVES 4 ———

450 g (1 lb) red onions or Spanish onions, skinned
60 ml (4 tbsp) hazelnut oil
30 ml (1 level tbsp) fresh marjoram or oregano, torn or chopped
700 g (1½ lb) red-skinned potatoes
2.5 ml (½ level tsp) sea salt
freshly ground nutmeg or black pepper
1 green pepper, halved lengthways, seeded and sliced

5–6 size 2 eggs, beaten (depending upon size and depth of dish)
1 lemon, grated zest, juice
45 ml (3 level tbsp) strained natural yogurt
50 g (2 oz) hazelnuts, toasted or roasted, coarsely chopped
25 g (1 oz) Pecorino, strong farmhouse Cheddar, or Cabrales cheese

67

Slice the onions into 6 mm (¼ inch) slices. Put them into large, 30 cm (12 inch) oval flameproof pan with the oil and herbs. Fry over moderate heat for 8–10 minutes, until onions are softened and the herb smells aromatic. Remove from pan.

Slice the onions into 6 mm (¼ inch) slices. Put them into a large, 30 cm (12 inch) oval flameproof pan with the oil and herbs. Fry over moderate heat for 8–10 minutes, until onions are softened and the herb smells aromatic. Remove from pan.

Uncover the dish and scatter over the green pepper strips. Whisk the lemon zest, juice and eggs together with the yogurt until blended but not frothy, and pour this evenly over the surface of the dish to completely cover it. Scatter on the hazelnuts and grate the cheese directly onto the egg layer.

Return the dish to the oven, increase the heat to 200°C/400°F/Gas Mark 6 and bake, uncovered, for about 8–10 minutes or until creamy and set but not dry.

Serve in big wedges, accompanied by some crisp, colourful salads (watercress, chicory, purslane and trevise or radicchio would taste good), in a lemony dressing. A good Rioja or Barbaresco would not be unwelcome (if you are not so purist that you feel the taste of lemon will utterly destroy your wine!). A mousse, sorbet, fresh fruit salad or syllabub could finish the meal.

TARTE URSULAINE

THIS INTERESTING semi-savoury tart consists of a blanket of white cheese, yogurt and egg white covering the layered fruit and vegetables. The edges of the pastry and the leeks and nuts on top may become slightly dark, which tastes delicious. The name for this dish comes partly from the combination of apple, tomato and onion flavours (a time-honoured combination from an Ursula of my acquaintance) and the fact that the white 'veil' of egg, yogurt and cheese resembles an Ursuline nun's wimple.

—— SERVES 4 ——

PASTRY:
175 g (6 oz) plain, unbleached flour
50 g (2 oz) soft dark brown sugar
75 g (3 oz) butter, at room temperature
3 size 2 egg yolks
2.5 ml ($\frac{1}{4}$ tsp) rich soy sauce

FILLING:
450 g (1 lb) apples, (Cox's Orange, Discovery, russets)
350 g (12 oz) tomatoes

3 size 2 egg whites
300 ml ($\frac{1}{2}$ pint) strained natural yogurt
2.5 ml ($\frac{1}{2}$ level tsp) salt
225 g (8 oz) white firm cheese, (e.g. Dunlop, Wensleydale or Caerphilly)
50 g (2 oz) shelled hazel nuts, chopped or grated coarsely
50 g (2 oz) shelled cashew nuts, chopped
1 large leek, shredded finely

Make the pastry by mixing together the flour and sugar and cutting or rubbing in the butter until the mixture resembles coarse breadcrumbs. Beat the yolks with the soy sauce and stir into the dry ingredients. Knead into a firm dough. Cover and chill for 30 minutes (or fast chill in the freezer for 5 minutes, if time is a consideration).

Roll or press out, (the mixture is rather hard to handle easily), to line the base and sides of a 25 cm (10 inch)-diameter quiche dish, or an equivalent-sized pie plate with rim.

Halve, core and slice half the apples into the base. Cover with half the tomatoes, sliced thickly. Repeat the apple and tomato layering, until all are used.

Lightly whisk the egg whites and gently blend with a little of the yogurt. Fold into the remaining yogurt and season well with salt. Stir in the grated cheese, then pour or spoon this mixture over the tart to cover the contents.

Scatter over the hazel nuts, cashew nuts and finally arrange the thin leek rings in a decorative border.

Bake near the top of the oven at 190°C/375°F/Gas Mark 5 for 35–40 minutes, or until the pastry is crisp and the tart smells cooked. Serve in large slices, hot, warm or cool.

A crisp green bean and iceberg lettuce salad with a coarse grain mustard dressing would be an appropriate accompaniment, and some good red wine (perhaps a Cabernet Sauvignon, whether European, Californian or Antipodean). Follow this course, perhaps with a chocolate sorbet (see page 146), good coffee and some small sweetmeats of your own choice.

Tudor Latticed Pie

A SPLENDID OFFERING which has something of the feeling of a portcullis about its domed and decorative top. This brings to my mind's eye castles and towers, and prunes, leeks, eggs, almonds and Wensleydale are certainly English enough. The surprise addition is tender avocado which becomes a little astringent as it cooks—a curious phenomenon. Don't be alarmed that the parsley darkens as the pie bakes, (more should be thrown over it at serving time)—the texture is quite appealing.

——— SERVES 4 ———

900 g (2 lb) leeks, both green and white
    parts, prepared and washed
50 ml (2 fl oz) light ale or lager
150 ml (5 fl oz) single cream
375 g (13 oz) good quality prunes,
    (Pruneaux d'Agen or Californian
    prunes), stoned
50 g (2 oz) whole blanched almonds
4 hard boiled eggs, shelled and halved
    lengthways

100 g (4 oz) white Wensleydale cheese,
    cubed
1 ripe avocado, skinned, stoned and cubed
225 g (8 oz) prepared puff pastry, chilled
60 ml (4 level tbsp) chopped parsley
1.25 ml ($\frac{1}{4}$ level tsp) powdered cloves
a little egg yolk and milk (for egg wash)

TO SERVE:
extra chopped parsley

Slice leeks into 2.5 cm (1 inch) chunks. Drain, leaving on the water that clings. Put them, with enough boiling salted water to quarter-cover them, into a large saucepan, bring to the boil, reduce heat and simmer for 4–6 minutes, or until barely tender. Drain, reserving cooking liquid.

Put approximately one quarter of the leeks with the ale and the cream into a food processor or blender and process or blend to a purée, adding enough of the cooking liquid to give a creamy texture. Put aside.

Insert an almond (or two) into each prune.

In a 23 cm (9 inch)-diameter deep pie plate, layer half the leek chunks, with the prunes, eggs, (cut sides down), cheese and avocado cubes. Cover with the remaining leek chunks, mounding the pie up in an even curve. Pour over the puréed leek, ale and cream mixture, and sprinkle with an even layer of parsley and cloves.

Roll out the pastry to a rectangle approximately 25 × 40 cm (10 × 16 inches). Using a cleaver, cut 16 even-sized strips long enough to cover the dish.

Moisten the rim of the dish and cover the rim with strips of pastry. Lattice the pie with 5 strips laid in one direction, and another 5 at right angles. Moisten ends and press firmly to seal at edges. Brush egg wash on the rim pastry, then cover the pastry ends with more strips, pressing them down firmly to make a secure seal. Chill for 30 minutes (pastry ends still untrimmed). Trim pastry ends. Brush pastry again with egg wash.

Bake in an oven at 230°C/450°F/Gas Mark 8 for 20–25 minutes or until pastry is dark, crisp and puffed. (Cover part way through with absorbent kitchen paper if a lighter effect is preferred.) Scatter over freshly chopped parsley.

PERSONALITY PASTA

MAKING HOMEMADE PASTA

Pasta is best made using a heavy Italian pasta machine which is operated by hand. (It can also be shaped, rolled and cut entirely by muscle power, a rolling pin and patience—but this process takes longer.) With a little practice you will find the skill of pasta-making deeply therapeutic and creatively soothing! It also becomes quick: using a food processor to make the dough and a pasta machine to shape and cut it, we managed to make enough for 4 servings in under 15 minutes, easily, time after time. Once you have made your own pasta successfully, and experienced its texture and flavour you will find it hard to buy pasta. Dress and serve hand-made pasta like this with very little ceremony: it is too good not to simply enjoy straight with the tiniest of salad garnishes, perhaps.

CARDAMOM AND SAFFRON PASTA

(Illustrated facing page 33)

CARDAMON SCENTS this fresh, homemade pasta with a pungent, clean taste and saffron bestows its golden blessings. It is memorable for both these qualities and the fact that you will never find it on sale anywhere, though some creative young chef, for all I know, may have 'discovered' it at the same time as I. (If so, I want to go to his restaurant to eat!) This is a really glorious midsummer dish—full of colour and freshly appealing to the eye. If you can't get pot marigold flowers, nasturtiums make a good substitute. Do toss in the leaves and flowers at the very last minute and serve immediately.

SERVES 4

500 mg (4 sachets) pure, good quality
  saffron, powdered or 5 ml (1 level tsp)
  strands
15 green cardamom pods, crushed, seeds
  extracted
225 g (8 oz) strong plain white flour
2.5 ml ($\frac{1}{2}$ level tsp) salt
2 size 2 eggs

TO SERVE:
25 g (1 oz) unsalted butter, cut in tiny
  cubes
dandelion, curly endive or feuilles de chêne
  (oak leaf lettuce) leaves and pot
  marigold flowers, (optional)

Put the saffron, cardamom seeds, flour and salt into the bowl of the food processor. Break in the eggs. Process in short bursts until the mixture resembles crumbs.

With the processor motor running gradually add the water through the feed tube. Process until clumps begin to form (it should be sufficient to make the pasta form a cohesive ball). Remove from the food processor, roll generously in flour, divide the dough in quarters and cling film, keeping 1 unwrapped ready to roll out.

Set the rollers of the pasta machine to their widest setting and feed the unwrapped, floured and flattened portion of dough through the rollers. It will emerge somewhat more flattened.

Flour the pasta again very well on both sides and fold both ends over each other towards the middle to overlap. Corrugate it firmly with the fingertips or the side of the hand.

Feed the dough, with the folded edges towards the sides of the machine, through the rollers and then repeat the process flouring, folding and corrugating the dough as before. Repeat this process 5 or 6 times until the dough feels satiny-smooth. You are now ready to thin the dough. From now on do not fold the dough into thirds.

Decrease the space between the rollers by 1 notch and feed the sheet of dough through the rollers again. Continue to decrease the space between the rollers by 1 notch each time. If the dough feels at all sticky, dust with flour on both sides. Notice that the dough is stretching and thinning. When you get to the last but 2 notches on the machine, the sheet of dough should measure about 60 cm (24 inches) in length. Keep the completed sheet aside, hanging it on a pasta or other rack.

Repeat processes with the 3 reserved balls of dough, to yield 4 even lengths of rolled out pasta.

To make the noodles, feed each pasta sheet through the wide cutters, reaching with your other hand to catch the pasta and loop it out of the way as it emerges. Hang the pasta again over a bar or rack.

Drop the pasta gradually into at least 3.4 litres (6 pints) of fast boiling water. Bring back to the boil. Partially cover, and cook for $3\frac{1}{2}$ minutes, testing to see if it is cooked to your liking.

Drain the pasta well and shake. Tip it quickly into a heated serving plate or bowl with the butter. Shake, toss in some of the salad leaves of your choice, strewing marigold petals over at the very last minute.

JEALOUSY NOODLES WITH ENOKI DRESSING

I HAVE been reliably informed that in Chinese 'to eat vinegar' means 'to be jealous'. In this recipe, homemade, aniseedy noodles (you'll need a pasta making machine) are tossed with a vegetable dressing which is finished off by a sharp but judicious dash of jealousy! The dressing balances the mild sweetness of the noodles. Chinese five spice powder tastes so right upon the tongue that it is easy to feel that it is only *one* flavour. However, it should be used very fresh—buy small amounts from a reliable supplier. Enoki mushrooms are delicate mushrooms, beautiful to look at and to eat.

———— SERVES 4 ————

225 g (8 oz) strong plain white flour
2.5 ml ($\frac{1}{2}$ level tsp) salt
10 ml (2 level tsp) five spice powder
2 size 2 eggs
30 ml (2 tbsp) water (as needed)

DRESSING:
15 ml (1 tbsp) peanut oil
5 ml (1 tsp) dark sesame oil
75 g (3 oz) spring onions, prepared, finely
   chopped
4–6 sticks celery, thinly sliced on the
   diagonal
225 g (8 oz) broccoli, sliced into tiny florets
125 g (4 oz) unpeeled, cubed cucumber
15 ml (1 tbsp) light soy sauce
30 ml (2 tbsp) white wine vinegar
125 g (4 oz) enoki mushrooms (optional)

Put the flour, salt and spice into the bowl of the food processor. Break in the eggs, process in short bursts until the mixture resembles crumbs.

With the processor motor running, add a little water, 2.5 ml ($\frac{1}{2}$ tsp) at a time through the feed tube. Continue to add and to process until the mixture begins to form clumps (the dough should form a cohesive ball). Remove from the food processor, roll generously in flour, divide the dough into 4. Wrap 3 pieces in cling film and reserve until ready for use. Keep 1 unwrapped ready to roll out.

Set the rollers of the pasta machine to their widest setting and feed the unwrapped, floured and flattened portion of dough through the rollers. It will emerge more flattened.

Flour the pasta again on both sides and fold both ends over each other towards the middle to overlap. Corrugate it firmly with the fingertips or the side of the hand.

Feed the dough, with the folded edges towards the sides of the machine, through the rollers and then repeat the process flouring, folding and corrugating the dough as before. Repeat this process 5 or 6 times until the dough feels satiny-smooth. You are now ready to thin the dough. From now on do not fold the dough into thirds.

Decrease the space between the rollers by 1 notch and feed the sheet of dough through the rollers again. Continue to decrease the space between the rollers by 1 notch each time. If the dough feels at all sticky, dust with flour on both sides. Notice that the dough is stretching and thinning. When you get to the last but 2 notches on the machine the sheet of dough should measure about 60 cm (24 inches) in length. Put the completed sheet aside.

Repeat the processes with the reserved 3 balls of dough, to yield 4 even lengths of rolled out pasta. Lay these out flat in one layer, loosely covered and well-floured.

To make the noodles, feed each pasta sheet through the wide cutters, reaching with your other hand to catch the pasta and loop it out of the way as it emerges.

Drop the pasta gradually into at least 3.4 litres (6 pints) of fast boiling water. Bring back to the boil. Partially cover, and cook for $\frac{1}{2}$–1 minute (from really fresh), testing to see if it is cooked to your liking.

Drain the noodles well and shake. Tip them into a heated serving plate or bowl and keep hot.

Quickly heat the 2 oils together in a wok or large heavy-based frying pan. Add the onions, celery, broccoli and cucumber, stir-fry, reducing the heat so that the vegetables become brilliantly green and crisp and hot (about 1–2 minutes). Add the soy sauce and the vinegar all at once, shaking the pan to mix all elements together and coat them. Toss the hot dressing over the noodles and serve while the vegetables are at their best. Scatter little bunches of enoki mushrooms (thin-stemmed, miniature white mushrooms) over all.

A bowl of baby sweetcorn on the cob, with fresh coriander could accompany this dish. This course could be followed by a rich aubergine purée of some kind with crisp breads or crisp crackers to accompany it, then a mousse, sorbet, parfait or ice. Fresh lichees and some scented tea would round off the meal well.

73

WHOLEWHEAT TAGLIATELLE WITH SAUCE PUTTANARA

MAKING WHOLEWHEAT tagliatelle is pleasing (the speckled texture and colour remind one of straw and birds' eggs and other earthy things) as long as the mixture is kept fairly moist, otherwise it is fiendishly difficult to roll out. This particular sauce (as may be ascertained from its name) is not a pure and unsullied sauce but is a sauce of my own invention; a sort of 'interfered with' version of pesto. Though one should not tamper with the classic sauces, one often does and I think this one is worthy of a fling. Make it in a blender while the pasta cooks, so it is vividly alive and tasty with freshness. Warn your guests about the garlic! Passato can be bought (in cartons) or made at home in the blender or processor. If no fresh basil can be found use decent quality pesto instead (preferably homemade, from late summer basil, and stored in sealed pots in a refrigerator).

——— SERVES 4 ———

PASTA:
225 g (8 oz) stoneground wholewheat,
  (wholemeal), 100% extraction flour
2.5 ml (½ level tsp) salt
1 size 1 egg
10 ml (2 tsp) olive oil
30 ml (2 tbsp) water (as needed)
10 fresh basil leaves (minimum) (or 60 ml/
  2 level tbsp) pesto

SAUCE:
2 garlic cloves, skinned and crushed
10 fresh basil leaves (minimum) (or 60 ml
  (2 level tbsp) pesto)
25 g (1 oz) toasted pinenuts
450 ml (¾ pint) passato (or freshly puréed
  tomatoes)
225 g (8 oz) fresh, young spinach leaves,
  finely shredded
150 ml (¼ pint) fruity olive oil (not
  necessarily pure virgin type)
75–100 g (3–4 oz) Parmesan (Grana)
  cheese freshly grated

Put the flour, salt and eggs into the bowl of the food processor and blend, in short bursts, until the mixture resembles crumbs.

Mix the oil and water together. With the processor motor running, add a little liquid (2.5 ml (½ tsp) at a time). Continue to add and to process until the dough begins to form clumps—it should form a cohesive ball. Remove the dough from the food processor, roll generously in flour, divide the dough into 4, wrap 3 in cling film and reserve until ready for use. Keep 1 unwrapped, ready to roll out.

Set the rollers of the pasta machine to their widest setting and feed the unwrapped, floured and flattened portion of dough through the rollers. It will emerge somewhat more flattened.

Flour the pasta again on both sides and fold both ends over each other towards the middle to overlap. Corrugate it firmly with the fingertips or the side of the hand.

Feed the dough, with the folded edges towards the sides of the machine, through the rollers and then repeat the process flouring, folding and corrugating the dough as before. Repeat this process 5 or 6 times until the dough feels satiny-smooth. You are now ready to thin the dough. From now on do not fold the dough into thirds.

Decrease the space between the rollers by 1 notch and feed the sheet of dough through the rollers again. Continue to decrease the space between the rollers by 1 notch each time. If the dough feels at all sticky, dust with flour on both sides. Notice that the dough is stretching and thinning. When you get to the last but 2 notches on the machine the sheet of dough should measure about 60 cm (24 inches) in length. Keep the completed sheet aside.

Repeat the processes with the 3 reserved balls of dough, to yield 4 even lengths of rolled out pasta. Lay these out flat in one layer, loosely covered and floured well.

To make the noodles, feed each pasta sheet through the narrow cutters, reaching with your other hand to catch the pasta and loop it out of the way as it emerges.

Drop the pasta gradually into at least 3.4 litres (6 pints) of fast boiling water. Bring back to the boil. Partially cover, and cook for $2-2\frac{1}{2}$ minutes, testing to see if it is cooked to your liking.

Drain the pasta well and shake into a heated serving plate or bowl. Keep hot.

To make the sauce put the ingredients, in order, into a blender or food processor and process to get a rough, grainy sauce in which the textures of the original ingredients are still slightly discernible. Pour directly over the pasta, stir quickly. Serve without too much dallying. (If wished, keep back a few of the pretty shield-like spinach leaves for decoration.)

This quantity would serve 8 as an hors d'oeuvre before a main dish, and for speed, pasta asciutta such as fusilli, fusilli bucati, bozzoli or spirale could be used in place of homemade pasta. Follow timings on packs.

Fresh Orange Zested Fettucine with Creamy Peanut Dressing

(Illustrated facing page 33)

T HESE NOODLES emerge from the pasta machine a lovely pastel orange, firm textured and decorative. Once cooked they are subtle and delicious. Their sweetness almost calls out for soured cream, crème fraîche or clotted cream (all of which I occasionally enjoy) but if you prefer a low-fat dressing, use a good quality creamy but low fat natural yogurt. (One Greek brand, made of sheeps' milk has only 6 per cent fat yet a wondrous texture.) With the dressed pasta I serve a piquant peanut sauce, not unlike a type of Indonesian satay sauce. Each diner stirs in their sauce on the plate, so the flavours all remain excellently fresh and clear.

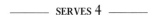

——— SERVES 4 ———

PASTA:
225 g (8 oz) strong plain white flour
2.5 ml (½ level tsp) salt
30 ml (2 level tbsp) freshly shredded
  orange zest
2 size 2 eggs
30 ml (1 tbsp) orange juice, freshly
  squeezed
30 ml (1 tbsp) water (plus another 10 ml
  (2 tsp) added as needed)

DRESSING:
60 ml (4 level tbsp) coarse peanut butter
60 ml (4 tbsp) boiling water
60 ml (4 tbsp) orange juice, freshly
  squeezed
1.25 ml (¼ level tsp) fresh red chilli, finely
  chopped
5 ml (1 level tsp) tomato purée
15 ml (1 level tbsp) roasted peanuts,
  roughly chopped

TO SERVE:
150 ml (¼ pint) cream of your choice (see
  above) or thick, low fat natural yogurt

Put the flour, salt and zest into the bowl of the food processor. Break in the eggs. Process in short bursts until the mixture resembles crumbs.

With the processor motor running, gradually add the measure of orange juice and the measure of water. Continue to add and to process until the dough begins to form clumps—it should form a cohesive ball, adding the extra teaspoon of liquid if needed. Remove pasta from the food processor, roll generously in flour, divide the dough into 4 portions, wrap 3 in cling film and reserve until ready for use.

Set the rollers of the pasta machine to their widest setting and feed the unwrapped, floured and flattened portion of dough through the rollers. It will emerge somewhat more flattened.

Flour the pasta again on both sides and fold both ends over each other towards the middle to overlap. Corrugate it firmly with the fingertips or the side of the hand.

Feed the dough, with the folded edges towards the sides of the machine, through the rollers and then repeat the process flouring, folding and corrugating the dough as before. Repeat this process 5 or 6 times until the dough feels satiny-smooth. You are now ready to thin the dough. From now on do not fold the dough into thirds.

Decrease the space between the rollers by 1 notch and feed the sheet of dough through the rollers again. Continue to decrease the space between the rollers by 1 notch each time. If the dough feels at all sticky, dust with flour on both sides. Notice that the dough is stretching and thinning. When you get to the last notch on the machine the sheet of dough should be very thin, measuring about 125 cm (50 inches) in length. Keep the completed sheet aside, hanging it on a pasta or other rack.

Repeat the processes with the 3 reserved balls of dough, to yield 4 even lengths of rolled out pasta.

To make the fettucine, feed each pasta sheet through the wide cutters, reaching with your other hand to catch the pasta and loop it out of the way as it emerges.

Drop the pasta gradually into a least 3.4 litres (6 pints) of fast boiling water. Bring back to the boil. Partially cover, and cook for $2-2\frac{1}{2}$ minutes, testing for doneness sooner, as liked.

Drain the noodles well and shake. Tip them back into a heated plate or bowl. Add the dressing of cream or yogurt, toss well.

Blend all the peanut dressing ingredients to make a fairly smooth consistency.

Allow each diner a spoonful of the peanut sauce. It should be stirred in just before being eaten, which should happen without delay.

This quantity would serve 8 as an hors d'oeuvre before a main dish.

With the pasta (or following it), a salad of triangles of fresh pineapple, fresh dates, chicory and watercress would be very pleasant. Good crusty bread is always welcome. Nuts, some strong-flavoured cheese, and crisp celery could end this meal, and some really freshly made expresso coffee.

MOREL AND PARMIGIANO PASTA

(Illustrated facing page 33)

THE TINIEST quantity of dried morels (wild mushrooms) transform this quickly made fresh pasta into a considerable delicacy. Good aged cheese sharpens the edge of the effect. Some of this is grated freshly and incorporated into the pasta, while the remainder is crumbled or flaked into the sauce (which is made on the plate—no cooking) and tossed into baby, shield-shaped, smoothest-of-green spinach leaves (sometimes called pousse épinards). This type of spinach can be expensive, so I have suggested other young green salad stuffs as an alternative, if you are not feeling rich. On the other hand, if you consider what you've already avoided paying, (no steak, no chops, no chicken) the spinach and the utterly delicious Mascarpone and Grana cheeses will seem sensible expenditures. Vegetarian thinking, it seems to me, is not merely about lentils, tofu and carrot juice; it concerns, hopefully, values, and balance, on many levels. Most good Italian delicatessens will stock the essential constituents of this recipe. The greenery is best bought from specialist greengrocer or an enlightened supermarket and must be eaten fresh.

———— SERVES 4 ————

PASTA:
15 g (½ oz) dried morels, finely crumbled
120 ml (4 fl oz) warm water (later reduced to 30 ml (2 tbsp)) for the sauce
25 g (1 oz) Parmesan (Grana) cheese
200 g (7 oz) strong plain white flour
2.5 ml (½ level tsp) salt
2 size 2 eggs

TO SERVE:
15 g (½ oz) unsalted butter
25 g (1 oz) Parmesan (Grana), crumbled
125 g (4 oz) Mascarpone (or other delicate creamy cheese)
125 g (4 oz) baby spinach leaves, pousse épinards or young, green salad stuffs, i.e. dandelion, chicory, mâche, or very tender red root spinach, torn into pieces

Crumble the morels into the water. Simmer gently, covered, for 5 minutes. Strain. Keep mushrooms aside. Reduce mushroom liquor to 30 ml (2 tbsp) only. Cool.

Put the grater attachment into the food processor and grate the cheese. Replace with the chopping blade and add the flour, salt, eggs and drained mushrooms to the food processor and blend in short bursts until the mixture begins to form clumps (the dough should form a cohesive ball).

Remove the mixture from the food processor, roll generously in flour, divide the dough into 4, wrap 3 in cling film and reserve until ready for use.

Set the rollers of the pasta machine to their widest setting and feed the unwrapped, floured and flattened portion of dough through the rollers. It will emerge somewhat more flattened.

Flour the pasta again well on both sides and fold both ends over each other towards the middle to overlap. Corrugate it firmly with the fingertips or the side of the hand.

Feed the dough, with the folded edges towards the sides of the machine, through the rollers and then repeat the process flouring, folding and corrugating the dough as before. Repeat this process 5 or 6 times until the dough feels satiny-smooth. You are now ready to thin the dough. From now on do not fold the dough into thirds.

Decrease the space between the rollers by 1 notch and feed the sheet of dough through the rollers again. Continue to decrease the space between the rollers by 1 notch each time. If the dough feels at all sticky, dust with flour on both sides. Notice that the dough is stretching and thinning. When you get to the last but 1 notch on the machine the sheet of dough should measure about 75–90 cm (30–36 inches) in length. Keep the completed sheet aside, hanging it on a pasta or other rack.

Repeat the processes with the 3 reserved balls of dough, to yield 4 even lengths of rolled out pasta.

To make the noodles, feed each pasta sheet through the narrow cutters, reaching with your other hand to catch the pasta and loop it out of the way as it emerges.

Drop the pasta gradually into at least 3.4 litres (6 pints) of fast boiling water. Bring back to the boil. Partially cover, and cook for 2 minutes, testing for doneness sooner, as liked.

Drain the pasta well and shake. Heap it on a large, heated serving plate, with the butter, reserved mushroom liquor, the Mascarpone, the Grana and the little leaves. Toss together to mix and eat without delay, while pasta, sauce and leaves are at their quintessential best.

This quantity would serve 8 as an hors d'oeuvre before a main dish.

A good St Amour, or similar red wine would be a sympathetic companion to this dish, and some light, crisp French bread from a really good baker, to break and eat with the pasta.
Follow, if liked, with globe artichokes filled with a fresh herb vinaigrette (or an orange yogurt mousseline), then some brie or camembert and some fresh blueberries or cherries.

79

PURSLANE AND PARSLEY FETTUCINE

(Illustrated facing page 33)

PURSLANE (the *portulaca* plant, also known as pigweed, porcellana and pourpier, depending upon the nationality of the countries exporting it, or the greengrocers who stock it,) grows wild and can often be found in hot places. It is good in salads, (hot or cold) or, as here, as a purée to colour and flavour pasta. When bought in the immature budding form it is often prohibitively expensive, but once it is full blown, it can be found (in large, shaggy, open bunches) in Greek and Cypriot greengrocers and bought for a song. Like many foods it is worth some effort to rediscover—once it was common fare, gathered by country people.

This pasta can be made (using a food processor and pasta machine) in under 20 minutes. The colour is curious speckly green. It tastes fresh and good. Since it contains greens, it needs little accompaniment: just a dusting of extra Parmesan (Grana), some cucumber, some butter or yogurt, fresh black pepper. With a pan of boiling salted water ready and waiting you'll have hand-made, fresh pasta ready to eat in under the half hour. Try it!

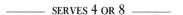

——— SERVES 4 OR 8 ———

25 g (1 oz) Parmesan (Grana) cheese
50 g (2 oz) fresh purslane, washed and
   well-dried
25 g (1 oz) flat leaf parsley, well-dried,
   chopped
225 g (8 oz) strong plain white flour
2.5 ml ($\frac{1}{2}$ level tsp) salt
2 size 2 eggs

TO SERVE:
25 g (1 oz) additional Parmesan (Grana),
   grated
50 g (2 oz) butter melted or 90 ml (6 level
   tbsp) natural yogurt
$\frac{1}{2}$ cucumber, peeled, halved lengthways,
   seeded, cross-cut and cut into crescents
2–3 budding heads of fresh purslane

Put the grater attachment into the food processor and grate the cheese. Keep aside. Replace with the chopping blade and add the purslane and parsley and process briefly, in short bursts, until finely chopped. (If no food processor is available, grate the cheese by hand and coarsely chop the green leaves.)

Put the cheese, green leaves, flour, salt and eggs into the food processor and blend, in short bursts, until the mixture begins to form clumps (the dough should form a cohesive ball).

Remove from the food processor, roll generously in flour, divide the dough into 4 portions, wrap 3 in cling film and reserve until ready for use, (keeping 1 unwrapped ready to roll out).

Set the rollers of the pasta machine to their widest setting and feed the unwrapped, floured and flattened portion of dough through the rollers. It will emerge somewhat more flattened.

Flour the pasta again very well on both sides and fold both ends over each other towards the middle to overlap. Corrugate it firmly with the fingertips or the side of the hand.

Feed the dough, with the folded edges towards the sides of the machine, through the rollers and then repeat the process flouring, folding and corrugating the dough as before.

Repeat this process 5 or 6 times until the dough feels satiny-smooth. You are now ready to thin the dough. From now on do not fold the dough into thirds.

Decrease the space between the rollers by 1 notch and feed the sheet of dough through the rollers again. Continue to decrease the space between the rollers by 1 notch each time. If the dough feels at all sticky, dust with flour on both sides. Notice that the dough is stretching and thinning. When you get to the last but 2 notches on the machine, the sheet of dough should measure about 60 cm (24 inches) in length. Keep the completed sheet aside, hanging it on a pasta or other rack.

Repeat the processes with the 3 reserved balls of dough, to yield 4 even lengths of rolled out pasta.

To make the fettucine, feed each pasta sheet through the wide cutters, reaching with your other hand to catch the pasta and loop it out of the way as it emerges.

Drop the pasta gradually into at least 3.4 litres (6 pints) of fast boiling water. Bring back to the boil. Partially cover, and cook for $3\frac{1}{2}$ minutes, testing for doneness sooner, as liked.

Drain the pasta well and shake. Tip it quickly into a heated serving plate or bowl. Add the dressing of grated cheese, butter or yogurt and cucumber crescents. Stir gently but quickly together. Add 1 or 2 decorative heads of purslane to the dish.

This quantity would serve 8 as an hors d'oeuvre before a main dish.

*H*ave plenty of freshly grated black pepper to hand, some good
*red wine and some crusty bread. This dish could be preceded by a clear soup or broth,
followed by some tomatoes in a little balsamic vinegar and good olive oil, then some
blue creamy Dolcelatte and some prickly pears or figs, or raisins and nuts to follow.*

PLOUGHMAN'S PASTA

W HO WOULD have guessed that such things as pickle could be added, with impunity, to homemade pasta? It means there is no end to the possibilities: piccalilli, peach, plum, apple, tomato, green tomato and goodness knows what else? The key requirement is that the pickle be flavourful.

——— SERVES 4 (OR 8) ———

225 g (8 oz) strong plain white flour
60 ml (4 level tbsp) good flavoured pickle
1 size 2 egg
30–45 ml (2–3 tbsp) water (as needed)
10 ml (2 tsp) olive oil
50 g (2 oz) butter

TO SERVE:
150 ml ($\frac{1}{4}$ pint) crème fraîche
30 ml (2 level tbsp) caraway seeds

Put the flour, pickle and egg into the food processor and process, in short bursts, until the mixture resembles crumbs.

Mix the water and the olive oil together. With the processor motor running, add a little liquid, 2.5 ml ($\frac{1}{2}$ tsp) at a time through the feed tube. Continue to add and to process until the mixture begins to form clumps (the dough should form a cohesive ball). Remove from the food processor, roll generously in flour, divide the dough into 4, wrap 3 in cling film and reserve until ready for use.

Set the rollers of the pasta machine to their widest setting and feed the unwrapped, floured and flattened portion of dough through the rollers. It will emerge somewhat more flattened. Flour the pasta again on both sides and fold both ends over each other towards the middle to overlap. Corrugate it firmly with the fingertips or the side of the hand. Feed the dough, with the folded edges towards the sides of the machine, through the rollers and then repeat the process flouring, folding and corrugating the dough as before. Repeat this process 5 or 6 times until the dough feels satiny-smooth.

Decrease the space between the rollers by 1 notch and feed the sheet of dough through the rollers again. Continue to decrease the space between the rollers by 1 notch each time. If the dough feels at all sticky, dust with flour on both sides. Notice that the dough is stretching and thinning. When you get to the last but 1 notch on the machine the sheet of dough should measure about 75–90 cm (30–36 inches) in length. Keep the completed sheet aside, hanging it on a pasta or other rack. Repeat the processes with the 3 reserved balls of dough, to yield 4 even lengths of rolled out pasta.

To make the noodles, feed each pasta sheet through the narrow cutters, reaching with your other hand to catch the pasta and loop it out of the way as it emerges. Drop the pasta gradually into at least 3.4 litres (6 pints) of fast boiling water. Bring back to the boil. Partially cover, and cook for 2–3 minutes, testing for doneness sooner, as liked.

Drain the pasta well. Toss butter (in small pieces) through the pasta and shake until it is gleaming and glossy, then add the cheese and onions. Toss again. Serve very hot.

The Vegetable Connection

Beets in Red Wine 'Au Nid'

I N THIS recipe, tender and sweet baked beetroot 'eggs' in a warm citrus-scented syrup are hidden within the marbled leaves of a head of almost-intact red chicory (radicchio). Any red leafed salad stuff could be substituted (e.g. red leafed lettuce, feuilles de chêne), but the effect is not quite as curious nor as pretty. Cool, slightly spiced cream and good bread and wine are the accompaniments to this appealing warm or cool salad, good for any season of the year.

—————— SERVES 4 ——————

700 g (1½ lb) even sized young beets,
* washed, topped and tailed*
50 ml (2 fl oz) boiling water
50 g (2 oz) caster sugar
150 ml (¼ pint) good red wine
1 orange, freshly shredded zest, squeezed
* juice*

boiling water
salt and freshly ground black pepper
1 large head 'marbled' radicchio, trimmed

TO SERVE:
150 ml (¼ pint) crème fraîche
30 ml (2 level tbsp) caraway seeds

Put the beets, with washing water still clinging, into a roasting bag, add 60 ml (2 fl oz) of boiling water, secure the bag loosely and place in a roasting pan in an oven preheated to 230°C/450°F/Gas Mark 8 for 1¼–1½ hours or until tender to the touch. Leave to stand for a few minutes, then remove, wrap each in absorbent kitchen paper and squeeze gently to remove the skin, leaving the beets clean.

Put the beets into a saucepan big enough to hold them in one layer. Add the sugar, orange zest and juice, wine, and enough boiling water to almost cover. Bring to simmering, loosely covered, and cook for 20 minutes more. Leave to cool. Halve the beets and season well. Retain the syrup.

Open the leaves of the radicchio (cut out and discard a cone-shaped section of the base) and put the leaves into a pretty bowl, upright. Push the beets down between the layers of the 'nest' until all are used. Pour over the warm syrup. Put the crème fraîche in a bowl, sprinkle with caraway and serve alongside.

ASPARAGUS CASKETS WITH CHERVIL CREAM

THERE IS a simple French asparagus dish which Alice B. Toklas, in her famous cookbook of the same name, describes as 'a gastronomic feast. And a thing of beauty.' The recipe employed 'tiny young spring asparagus, very like the wild ones.' I find that this fresh, very straight slim asparagus, often called 'sprue', (it is the size of a little finger, or thereabouts), tastes good, costs less and is often more available and affordable than the huge bunches. According to a reputable grower this aparagus is shy (apparently it may peep out of the ground then, if the time is not auspicious, withdraw until a more suitable time). Asparagus should always be taken without delay to the pot. Which brings me to another point: asparagus steamers are decorative and fine (for those who own them) but I have personally found asparagus cooks just as well when laid horizontally in one layer in boiling salted water (with the points all facing one direction, of course, for efficient draining) part-covered by lid or foil. It must always be cooked quickly, then drained and dried properly before being dressed for the table.

———— SERVES 4 ————

CASKETS:
450 g (1 lb) puff pastry, chilled
1 size 3 egg yolk
5 ml (1 level tsp) coarse grain Meaux mustard
5 ml (1 tsp) white wine, or white wine vinegar

FILLING:
900 g (2 lb) slim green asparagus spears
1 handful of fresh chervil (leaves and stalks)
30 ml (2 tbsp) Pernod, anise or Ricard
125 g (4 oz) fromage frais or fromage blanc battu
freshly ground salt
freshly ground black pepper

Roll out the pastry to 40 × 30 cm (16 × 12 inches), large enough for 12.5 cm (5 inch) saucers to be cut around with a knife, to make 6 circles. Arrange these evenly on a wetted baking sheet. Brush the tops with the mixed yolk, mustard and wine or wine vinegar.

Using a sharp-bladed knife, make a series of 5 or 6 curving shallow slashes, radiating from the central point, on 4 of the pastry circles. Bake near the top of an oven at 230°C/450°F/ Gas Mark 8 for 10 minutes or until puffed, dark and crisp.

Heat 1 cm ($\frac{1}{2}$ inch) salted water into a large heavy, non-metal pan. Bring to the boil, cover. Snap off the less tender end from each asparagus spear and keep these aside (to use raw).

Place the asparagus, in one layer in the boiling water. Bring back to boiling. Part-cover, reduce the heat to a rolling simmer for 9–10 minutes (less if the asparagus is very fine).

Diagonally slice the better parts of the reserved stalk-ends into wafer-thin ovals, (or else grate on a coarse grater into shreds). Fold, together with the chervil and Pernod into the cheese to make a green sauce. Season to taste.

Remove the warm pastries from the oven and split each into two by lifting top from base. This makes 12 portions. Keeping the 4 decorated lids aside, spoon some sauce on to 8 pastry circles. Drain and dry the asparagus. Pile equal quantities on each circle.

Reassemble so that the 'casket' comprises 3 layers of pastry and 2 layers of sauce with asparagus. Enjoy whilst every part is at its best: the pastry hot and flaking, the sauce cool and fresh, the asparagus mellow and warm.

Chervil is not always available (though it makes a splendid window box herb) and though its aniseedy-delicacy is best in this recipe, young parsley could be used instead.

A really fragrant white burgundy, a Chardonnay, or a Sauvignon such as Quincy would be splendid with this dish.

CARNIVAL AUBERGINES

FAR QUICKER and easier than the usual Italian or Greek traditional stuffed aubergine technique, this decorative method ensures even cooking, simplicity and good fresh tastes. It looks good on its bed of green with cool fromage blanc alongside.

──── SERVES 4 ────

85

2 large purple aubergines, with green stems intact
fruity olive oil
1 large handful of fresh marjoram, oregano, or coriander

2 large marmande (or beefsteak) tomatoes
225 g (8 oz) Gruyère or Emmental cheese, in a rectangular block
chilled fresh lettuce leaves

Cut each aubergine and stem in half lengthways to give 4 perfect halves. Place these, lightly oiled on the cut surface, skin side upwards, on a baking tray.

Remove 6–8 small, parallel, wedge-shaped pieces from each halved aubergine (cutting almost to the base each time). Push some fresh herbs into each slash.

Slice the gruyère into 12 or 16 slices, then halve these crossways, to give 24 or 32 slices. Halve the tomatoes. Cut each half into 6 or 8 semi-circles.

Insert a piece of cheese and a tomato slice into each of the aubergine slashes, until all ingredients are used. Brush a little oil over exposed skin surfaces.

Bake in an oven at 190°C/375°F/Gas Mark 5 for 40–45 minutes or until the aubergines are just soft and the cheese and herbs smell aromatic. Serve sprinkled with salt and black pepper on a bed of green leaves or upon a chiffonade of lettuce (finely shredded lettuce).

GRILLED NECTARINES WITH HONEY-DRESSED WATERCRESS

Quickly-cooked nectarine halves taste fleshy and substantial when presented with a savoury stuffing upon a bed of dark, gleaming salt-sweet watercress. The secret is in the dressing: soy sauce and honey though maple syrup can be substituted for honey, if wished. If you can find it, use the lighter coloured soy. It is important to have all the ingredients ready before you start to grill the nectarines. This way you'll be sure you can dress the cress and serve the hot grilled fruit as soon as they're ready—otherwise the nectarines will begin to discolour.

───── SERVES 4 ─────

6 or 8 freestone nectarines (depending on size)
25 g (1 oz) shelled unblanched almonds, roughly chopped
75 ml (5 level tbsp) thick strained natural yogurt
175 g (6 oz) blue cheese (e.g. Pipo Crem', Dolcelatte, Gorgonzola), cubed
salt and freshly ground pepper
15 ml (1 tbsp) hazelnut or walnut oil

SALAD:
30 ml (2 tbsp) light soy sauce
30 ml (2 level tbsp) flower-scented honey or maple syrup
275 g (9 oz) watercress

TO SERVE:
freshly chopped parsley

Halve nectarines crossways, twist and remove the stones. Crush the stones, remove the kernels and use, if wished, as flavouring for the stuffing.

Mix the crushed kernels, almonds, yogurt and blue cheese together. Season well to taste.

Fill the fruit halves with a spoonful of the stuffing. Brush the exposed surfaces (and undercurves) of each fruit with a touch of the hazelnut or walnut oil and grill the fruit in their serving dish until the flesh wilts and the cheese begins to melt.

Blend the soy sauce and honey together (if the honey is thick then melt it gently over hot water). Wash and dry the cress. Divide into large, but manageable, sprigs. Just before serving, toss the cress in the dressing so that it is well coated.

Cover the serving dish with the salad. Carefully lift the grilled and bubbling fruit into a circle on the cress and serve without too much delay, as the tender flesh discolours upon standing.

FENNEL ZAKYNTHONIA

IDEALLY, REALLY pungent, sun-dried herbs, brought back from a favourite island in the Mediterranean, should perfume this dish, but substitute whatever herb you can find which is properly scented if good quality rígani (Greek oregano) is not available. Buy fennel with some green feathery tops, if possible. Good quality, fruity, dark green olive oil is needed here, and choose tomatoes with real flavour if you possibly can (a squeeze of tomato purée will help if these are unavailable).

————— SERVES 4 —————

2 garlic cloves, skinned and chopped
2 large or 4 small Florence fennel bulbs,
   halved lengthways (remove fronds)
45 ml (3 tbsp) fruity olive oil
450 g (1 lb) very ripe (preferably
   marmande) tomatoes
10 ml (2 level tsp) dried rígani (or oregano
   or marjoram)
450 ml (¾ pint) hot vegetable stock or
   water

225 g (8 oz) small conchiglie pasta shells
15 ml (1 level tbsp) tomato purée
extra vegetable stock or water

GARNISH:
25 g (1 oz) pinenuts
25 g (1 oz) sun-dried currants or raisins
freshly ground salt
freshly ground black pepper
fresh green fennel fronds

87

Put the garlic and halved fennel into a 1.7 litre (3 pint) casserole or flameproof lidded dish with the oil.

Chop the tomatoes and reduce to juice, pulp or purée in a juicer, food processor or blender. Add to the pan with the rígani, cover and braise in an oven, at 180°C/350°F/Gas Mark 4 for 1 hour, rearranging the fennel once.

Add the stock and pasta, stir to make sure the pasta is properly moistened, cover again and cook for a further 25–30 minutes, stirring gently halfway through to make sure the pasta is cooking evenly. Remove the lid, stir in the tomato purée (and a little extra stock, if needed) and return to the oven, uncovered.

Toast the pinenuts in a dry pan, shaking them over moderate heat until deep golden brown and very hot.

Serve the dish from the casserole with the reserved fennel fronds, chopped, toasted pinenuts and the currants on top.

*G*ood firm-textured Greek or Cypriot bread (particularly the
sesame-seed variety) is good served with this peasant dish, and some resinated Greek
red or white wine or Demestica if liked.
A bowl of black olives and some Feta cheese, then some watermelon might complete
this meal.

GARLANDED PACIFIC POTATO PUREE

(Illustrated facing page 97)

IMAGINE A smooth sweetish purée of spiced, orange-coloured sweet potato (some are pale in tone), almost identical in colour to pumpkin, around which are garlands of brilliant green broccoli, then a mirror of gleaming mange-tout peas. Green pumpkin seeds decorate the vegetables. This culinary 'set-piece' is easy and inexpensive to make and is memorable to eat. These long, pink-skinned tubers come in a variety of sizes and shapes and can usually be bought in Afro-Caribbean and West Indian stores or stalls, or in Greek, Cypriot, Oriental or Asian supermarkets. Even most giant supermarket chains stock them these days. In the Pacific they are called *kumara*.

——— SERVES 4 ———

*1.1 kg (2½ lb) orange-fleshed sweet
  potatoes (after peeling, yield will be
  1 kg (2¼ lb))
boiling water and sea salt
450 g (1 lb) young broccoli spears
225 g (8 oz) mange-tout peas
60 ml (4 level tbsp) fromage blanc (or
  other no-fat cheese)
10 ml (2 level tsp) cumin seeds, ground*

*TO SERVE:
30 ml (2 level tbsp) green pumpkin seeds
15 g (½ oz) butter, ghee or 15 ml (1 tbsp)
  olive oil, heated*

Peel the sweet potatoes as thinly as possible, then cross cut into 1 cm (½ inch) slices. Halve the larger ones crossways. Put the sweet potato into a heavy-based, lidded pan (preferably non-metal) and pour over sufficient boiling water to come half way up the sides. Add some salt. Bring back to a rapid boil, cover, reduce heat to a simmer and cook for 13–15 minutes or until a fork easily pierces the central fleshy part of the largest piece.

Halve the broccoli spears lengthways and remove tough ends. Divide any very large pieces into quarters, so all are of even size. Wash the mange-touts but do not remove the tops.

Drain the cooked potato (reserving the cooking liquid). Put the potato into a food processor. Process, pushing the mixture down from time to time between bursts, or whisk or mash using a potato masher, until a firm, smooth cream or purée is obtained. Do not overmix as it grows mushy with over handling. Mix in the fromage blanc and cumin.

Return the potato cooking water to the still-hot pan and add the broccoli, bring back to boiling and cook for 4–5 minutes. Throw in the mange-touts to steam on top of the broccoli. Cover and leave for a further 2–3 minutes.

Mound the hot purée upon a large, heated serving platter or dish, making decorative swirls using a spatula or spoon.

Drain the green vegetables. Arrange the broccoli around the purée in a ring. Scatter with the pumpkin seeds.

Surround the broccoli with mange-touts, drizzling over the melted butter, ghee or warm oil. Serve while the splendid construction looks its most brilliant, and encourage the diners to dip the peas and broccoli pieces into the purée rather as if it were a hot dip.

PEAS HAMMERSMITH

ONCE AT a Royal Academy banquet, when the eminent painter Joshua Reynolds was offered some overcooked and yellow peas, he is said to have suggested, lightheartedly, 'take them to Hammersmith . . . it's the way to Turnham Green.' In actual fact, baby fresh peas, when cooked for more than a brief period, especially in the presence of acid (wine, lemon juice, etc.) tend to discolour, but still taste delicious. Since baby peas can be eaten raw, all they really need is to be heated, in the most gentle, sweet and aromatic sauce, before being gratefully consumed. Here is a new look at the wonderful classic Petits Pois Frais à la Française, which is properly eaten with a spoon. Cos lettuce leaves provide a pretty border.

———— SERVES 4 ————

50 g (2 oz) butter
60 ml (4 tbsp) vegetable stock
4 or 6 bronze shallots, skinned and
*   quartered lengthways*
15 ml (1 level tbsp) caster sugar
2.5 ml (½ level tsp) salt
freshly ground pepper
700 g (1½ lb) fresh young shelled green peas

8 spring onions, halved lengthways and
*   crossways*
12–16 parsley stalks, tied together

TO SERVE:
30 ml (2 level tbsp) thick cream (or
*   fromage blanc battu)*
1 young cos lettuce, separated into leaves

89

Heat the butter, stock and quartered shallots in a pan with the sugar, salt and pepper, covered, until the shallots are tender.

Add the peas all at once, toss vigorously with the lid on over high heat until coated. Add the spring onions and parsley stalks. Cover tightly and cook over moderate heat, shaking the pan occasionally for 8–10 minutes or until the peas have heated through and are gleaming and moist (they do not need to be very soft).

Remove the parsley stalks, pour over the thick cream or fromage blanc battu, toss and serve surrounded by a circle of cos lettuce leaves to use as 'scoops'. Good French bread, fougasse, (or an earthy granary or wholemeal loaf in wafer thin slices), would work well with such tender and sweet tastes.

This dish must be served as a course in its own right. Precede (or
follow) it with a barely-set omelette containing mushrooms and fresh herbs, perhaps.
Afterwards a tomato and carrot salad dressed with orange juice and olive oil might
taste pleasant. Crisp young celery and a selection of goats' cheeses, e.g. blanc
(young), cendré (one which has been cured in cinders) and matured crottin (an
onomatopoeic name meaning 'droppings'), could bring an end to a delightful meal,
with some fresh dates, perhaps, or nuts, and coffee. Drink a lovely scented white wine,
perhaps a Graves, an Alsace wine, or a fruity Vouvray.

PALETTE OF POTATOES

(Illustrated opposite page 97)

I AM PLEASED to report that creamy, puréed potatoes are back in vogue! Real mashed potatoes, freshly combined with butter or cream, salt and pepper, please toddlers, teenagers, trend-setters and octogenarians alike! In this recipe a basic mixture gains various taste-enhancing additions, and these result in 5 separate colourful mounds, looking rather like an artist's palette.

———— SERVES 4 ————

2 kg (4 lb) good-flavoured potatoes, (e.g. King Edward or Desirée)
150 ml (¼ pint) vegetable stock
10 ml (2 level tsp) sea salt
freshly ground white pepper
60 ml (4 level tbsp) thick cream

ADDITION 1:
175 g (6 oz) raw baby beets, scrubbed and shredded
15 ml (1 level tbsp) freshly shredded orange zest
15 ml (1 tbsp) freshly squeezed orange juice

ADDITION 2:
225 g (8 oz) fennel, finely sliced
125 g (4 oz) spring or other cabbage greens, finely sliced
1 clove garlic, skinned and crushed

ADDITION 3:
125 g (4 oz) Pistachio Paste (see page 24) or chopped, shelled pistachios
25 g (1 oz) freshly chopped celery tops

ADDITION 4:
50 g (2 oz) Tapénaro (see page 20) or ready made tapénade

ADDITION 5:
125 g (4 oz) Fava Bean Cream (see page 114) or hummus
15 ml (1 level tbsp) tomato purée

TO SERVE:
50 g (2 oz) baby spinach leaves (pousse épinards) (optional)

Prepare the potatoes by peeling and cutting them into 1 cm (½ inch) cubes. Put them into a large turkey-roasting-size oven bag with the stock, sea salt and pepper. Loosely seal it, piercing it once (on top) then rest it on a baking sheet to 'oven steam' in the oven at 190°C/375°F/Gas Mark 5 for 60 minutes or until the liquid is almost completely absorbed.

Meanwhile prepare the 5 additional flavours or colours. They should be freshly cooked or prepared, shredded, puréed or mashed until each makes a smooth mixture. They should all be fully prepared and kept ready for combining at serving time. The beets should be well scrubbed before shredding using a food processor (shredder attachment) or coarse grater, then they should be tossed with the zest and juice. The fennel and cabbage should be cooked in a little stock or water (about 60 ml/4 tbsp), covered, over fierce heat until brilliant green, aromatic and bite-tender, approximately 4 minutes. They should then be processed with some crushed garlic. If you have no time to make the Pistachio Paste mix the chopped pistachios with some mayonnaise or yogurt. Similarly, if *tapénaro* is unavailable, use ready made tapénade. Hummus is a good substitute for Fava Bean Cream. Blend with the tomato paste.

When the potato is cooked, mash it, or use a potato ricer, or beat it using an electric whisk in a high-sided bowl with the cream. Do not use a food processor nor a blender—these render potato glue-like and unpleasant. It must be lump-free, smooth and yet hold its shape. Divide into 5 parts.

Stir the prepared purées into each quickly and thoroughly so that the mixture is still hot.

Serve each diner 5 separate scoops or moulds on heated plates, (use an ice cream scoop or a large serving spoon), trying to arrange them in a circle in this order: pink (beetroot), rosy (bean cream and tomato), tawny yellow (pistachio), green (fennel and cabbage), purply-black (*tapénaro*).

Scatter a handful of little spinach leaves at one side, rather like brushes on a palette.

Serve quickly before the food loses its charm (and its vitamins).

POTATOES HEDIARDINE

DISCREETLY TO one side of the great Madeleine in Paris, is one of my favourite browsing-places of the world—the old established firm of Hédiard. This recently updated but still timelessly classic store has imported some of the most wonderful fruit, vegetables, herbs, spices and syrups for decades. Their rows of rose petal jams, blackcurrant-scented teas, jewel-like sugared squares of fruit pastes, and exotic (and under-used) fruits and spices from Madagascar, Antilles, Ceylon and so on, as well as their famed selection of *piments* (peppers, their very own trademark) and a stunning wine cellar, makes them an education as well as a delight. I always buy one or other of their scented, spiced or herbed mustards at each visit. The one used in this simple recipe employs a 'three fruits' rosy mustard: one scented with cassis, framboise and tomato. Pomegranate seeds are incorporated as well as tossed over the surface at serving time. If no such mustard can be found use a really fine Dijon to which a purée or syrup of red fruits (homemade) has been added.

—— SERVES 4 ——

900 g (2 lb) small, new potatoes, scrubbed
175 g (6 oz) goats' cheese (e.g. crottin de
*   chavignol), chopped*
150 ml (5 fl oz) low fat natural yogurt

60 ml (4 level tbsp) rosy, fruited mustard
*   (or Dijon, scented with red fruits purée)*
2 pomegranates

Barely cover the potatoes with salted boiling water. Bring to the boil, reduce heat to a simmer and cook for 15–18 minutes or until just tender. Drain, return to the pan, uncovered, turn off heat. Blend the cheese, yogurt and mustard to a purée.

Quarter one of the pomegranates (give one quarter to each diner at serving time). Halve the other. Squeeze the juice from one half, using a lemon squeezer or juicer. Stir into the sauce. Remove the seeds from the other half. Halve the potatoes crossways. Dress with sauce and pile into a decorative bowl. Scatter with reserved pomegranate seeds.

SCENTED GOANESE POTATOES

I WAS LONG ago invited to partake of a delicious meal cooked by a flamboyant boy from Goa, whose family were all splendid cooks. In spite of all of the fascinating seafood, nut, vegetable and sweet dishes we tasted, the one, still, which lingers longest in my memory is a small dish containing hot, scented, golden potato pieces, in a moist and creamy sauce. This potato recipe has a little of that charm, though it seems banal by comparison.

SERVES 4

900 g (2 lb) Desirée, or other good
    potatoes, scrubbed
2 garlic cloves, skinned and sliced
2.5 cm (1 inch) of fresh root ginger,
    peeled, chopped
10 ml (2 level tsp) coriander seeds
1 small fresh red chilli, stem removed,
    finely sliced
10 ml (2 level tsp) turmeric powder
5 ml (1 level tsp) red paprika
5 ml (1 level tsp) cumin seeds
1 small onion, skinned and chopped
30 ml (2 tbsp) sunflower, safflower or
    mustard oil

225 g (8 oz) fresh okra (ladies fingers),
    trimmed but left whole
1 medium carrot, skinned and shredded
150 ml ($\frac{1}{4}$ pint) vegetable stock
freshly ground sea salt
150 ml ($\frac{1}{4}$ pint) natural yogurt
10–12 green cardamom pods, crushed and
    seeded

TO SERVE:
a few sprigs of fresh mint or coriander

Put the garlic, ginger, coriander, chilli, turmeric, paprika, cumin and onion into an electric grinder, or a pestle and mortar, and grind to a rough purée.

Heat the oil in a large frying pan, wok or sauté pan. Add the purée and stir until aromatic. Reduce the heat. Cut the potatoes into 1 cm ($\frac{1}{2}$ inch) cubes and add to the pan, stirring well until each piece is slightly coated.

Add the okra, carrot and stock. Stir gently, then cover and reduce the heat to a gentle simmer. Cook for 12–15 minutes or until the potato is tender, stirring once half-way through cooking time and topping up the liquid if necessary.

Season with salt to taste, and when the liquid is almost absorbed stir in the yogurt to blend with vegetables and sauce. Scatter cardamom seeds over all. Garnish with fresh mint or coriander sprigs. (If liked the potato can be packed into a mould for a few moments, pressed, then turned out onto a dish and surrounded with little fresh herb sprigs.)

*B*uttery spinach or Swiss chard, a tomato and onion salad and
some crisp papadoms would be pleasing accompaniments for this dish, along with
some hot seasonings of various kinds (particularly those using nuts).

POTATO HOTPOT ZEBRINE

Z EBRINE IS an Elizabeth David name (and enchanting description) for those delectable, slender, mauve-striped aubergines also sometimes known, less poetically, as 'Slim Jims'. Ethnic food stores and market stalls often stock these pretty vegetables. They contribute to this hotpot—a useful and pleasant supper for a wintry evening, made interesting with the additional flavours of mustard and whisky. Potatoes, however, are the mainstay of this homely offering and their shape and treatment both matter in the success of this recipe. A good dish to make and leave to cook, this needs a minimal amount of attention and no last minute effort whatsoever.

———— SERVES 4 ————

900 g (2 lb) potatoes (small and even in
   shape)
500 g (1 lb) zébrine or striped aubergines,
   sliced crossways 1 cm ($\frac{1}{2}$ inch) thick
30 ml (2 tbsp) olive oil
225 g (8 oz) celery, sliced finely
1 large onion, sliced 6 mm ($\frac{1}{4}$ inch) thick
1 large carrot, sliced 6 mm ($\frac{1}{4}$ inch) thick
handful of fresh parsley, chopped

sea salt and freshly ground pepper
45 ml (3 level tbsp) coarse grained mustard
375 ml (12 fl oz) vegetable stock
30 ml (2 tbsp) whisky
15 g ($\frac{1}{2}$ oz) butter, melted

TO SERVE:
extra parsley, finely chopped

93

Lightly oil a 1.5 litre ($2\frac{1}{2}$ pint) deep casserole or hotpot dish. Crossways halve enough potatoes to cover the top of the dish and keep aside, cut surfaces downwards.

Slice the remainder thickly, put into the casserole and cover with the aubergine slices, brushed on both sides with olive oil, the celery, onion and the carrot, seasoning each layer with salt, pepper and herbs to taste. Blend the mustard and whisky with the hot stock and pour over all. Cover with the reserved potato halves, curved sides upwards. Brush these with melted butter.

Cover the dish with lid or foil and cook in an oven preheated to 190°C/375°F/Gas Mark 5, for 2 hours, removing the lid after 1 hour to brown the potatoes. Garnish with extra parsley at serving time.

If no zébrines are available, use smallish, slender aubergines of the usual type. If aubergine 'eggs' (the spherical, white, Thai and Oriental variety—hence the alternative name, eggplant) are available, these could be quartered and used instead.

S erve with a green bean salad, with almonds and pinenuts, then
follow with fresh melon slices and perhaps a little saganaki—this is sliced, hard
cheese, lightly dusted with flour and pan-grilled in an oiled 2-handled frying pan,
until aromatic, crusty and near-melted (as is often served in little Greek tavernas at
the end of a meal).

TRUFFLED CHANTERELLES EN BARRIQUE

ALTHOUGH MANY serious-minded gastronomes might blench at the idea of an orange-zested brioche case filled with classic ingredients such as truffles, chanterelles, good red wine and cream, the combination is original and good. The buttery crust is moist and flavourful, a fitting receptacle for the wondrous filling tumbling out of the top. This is a dinner party dish for special occasions: the inclusion of a truffle tends to dictate the style. Fresh truffles should be selected, purchased, stored and sliced with love, care and attention and a really good supplier is important, as is a favoured wine merchant, when making this dish.

———— SERVES 4 ————

BRIOCHE GLAZE:
225 g (8 oz) ready-made (purchased)
  large brioche, (or a 450 g (1 lb) cottage
  loaf)
25 g (1 oz) butter
5 ml (1 level tsp) pink peppercorns
15 ml (1 level tbsp) freshly shredded
  orange zest
15 ml (1 tbsp) freshly squeezed orange juice

FILLING:
25 g (1 oz) butter
2 garlic cloves, skinned and chopped
50 g (2 oz) spring onions, sliced
1 medium onion, skinned and sliced
1 small, 50 g (2 oz), black truffle, thinly
  sliced
350 g (12 oz) fresh chanterelles, girolles,
  or champignons cleaned
60 ml (4 tbsp) red Bordeaux wine
75 ml (3 fl oz) thick, clotted cream
2.5 ml ($\frac{1}{2}$ level tsp) salt
45 ml (3 level tbsp) fresh, flat leaf parsley

To coat the brioche, heat the butter until melted, lightly crush the peppercorns and add with the zest and orange juice to the butter. Stir well.

Use a grapefruit knife, (or other short-bladed but serrated knife), held at a 45° angle to remove a cone shaped section from the brioche, leaving the shell about 2.5 cm (1 inch) thick. Retain the top, browned crusty section as lid, and slice off and discard the inner crumb section, thus making a hollow container. Enlarge the lower section by hollowing and discarding more crumbs if necessary, but make sure it remains a stout, substantial container.

Brush the inside and out of the brioche and the lid with the butter-pepper-orange glaze mixture.

Put the hollowed brioche with its lid on a baking sheet and allow it to become hot and crisp in an oven at 200°C/400°F/Gas Mark 6, for 8 minutes.

Put the second measure of butter, garlic, spring onions and onion into a heated frying pan and toss over moderate heat until wilted and tender. Add the truffle slices, cover the pan and shake over gentle heat for 1–2 minutes or until the truffle is aromatic, turning the slices gently.

Add the wine, the chanterelles or champignons, (sliced into halves or quarters, lengthways if they are large). Shake pan gently, turning the chanterelles in the wine-truffle sauce and then cover again and allow to cook through for 3–4 minutes.

Once the sauce, truffle and chanterelles are cooked and are aromatic and tender, add the cream, in small pieces, and shake the pan to melt and distribute it. Try to avoid stirring. Taste, adjust seasonings. Spoon the mushrooms, in their sauce, into the hot brioche case. Scatter parsley over all. Replace the lid at a rakish angle. Leave in the oven for a further 3–4 minutes, then serve.

COURGETTES PACIFICO

THIS IS a deliciously uncomplicated yet highly nutritious dish. Any tender member of the squash family would suffice e.g. yellow courgettes, young green courgettes, pattypan squashes, but do not use overgrown and watery marrows. Tropical fruits from the Pacific, pawpaw (papaya) and passion fruit are added. The emphasis is upon perfection and freshness of the ingredients. The combination of rather bland-tasting courgettes with a 'perfumed' sauce is fascinating to the palate. If you use coconut milk, you may need extra seasoning.

—— SERVES 4 ——

30 ml (2 tbsp) light-tasting olive oil or
  grapeseed oil
700 g (1½ lb) or 8 even-sized courgettes
  or other tender squash, halved
2 garlic cloves, skinned and chopped
2.5 cm (1 inch) piece of fresh ginger root,
  grated or shredded

4 ripe (wrinkled) passion fruit, halved
1 ripe pawpaw (papaya) skinned, seeded
  and sliced
125 ml (4 fl oz) white wine or coconut
  milk
salt
freshly ground pepper

Heat the oil in a large, heavy-based flameproof shallow casserole or lidded frying-pan, until very hot. Slice lengthways and add, cut face downwards, the courgettes (or crossways in the case of pattypans), without crowding the pan. Cook until browned. If necessary, do this in 2 stages. Carefully turn over the browned squashes, add the garlic and ginger and continue to cook for 1–2 minutes.

Scoop the pulp and seeds from the passion fruit and add to the pan with the pawpaw slices in an even layer. Add the white wine, cover, reduce heat and cook for 15 minutes. Season to taste.

Serve this with a bowl of rice, embellished with coconut cream,
nuts and spices of your own particular choice. Light fruity white wines taste good with
this dish.

SURPRISE STUFFED SPAGHETTI SQUASH

I F YOU grow spaghetti squash, then their curiosity will be no surprise. But for those who have no garden, do buy and try these egg-shaped delicacies whenever you find them. The individual servings are little masterpieces of understatement. At the centre of each perfect golden oval or half squash is hidden a cleverly disguised dressing, in pretty packaging. The central flesh of the spaghetti squash disintegrates, when forked into a tangle of tender fully edible shreds, looking (and feeling to the tongue) much like fine pasta.

———— SERVES 4 ————

2 spaghetti squashes (yellow, oval shaped)
boiling salted water

STUFFING:
4 leaves large Swiss chard (silver beet or 'blette')
120 ml (8 tbsp) Liptoi Fellegi (see page 25) cheese

Boil the 2 spaghetti squash, whole, barely covered with boiling salted water, with saucepan lid on, for 20 minutes turning them over half way through cooking time.

Meanwhile make the 'surprise': blanch the chard leaves in the same boiling water until they turn a brilliant dark green and the white stalks have become limp, not stiff. Refresh in iced water. Shake dry. Chop the stalks. Pile them in the centre of the 4 spread out leaves. Add 2 spoonfuls of Liptoi on to each leaf. Fold up the leaves to give 4 neat, flattish 'parcels', about 3.5 cm (1½ inch) square. Put these aside.

Dry the squashes and halve lengthways. Using 2 forks, pull the thread-like filaments apart enough to insert a green 'parcel' inside each. Cover again. Serve while the squashes are still hot and before the liptoi melts. Encourage diners to use knife and fork to tear the green and pink parcel open to become garnish and sauce, both.

A bold country soup could precede this dish, and a crisp leafy salad could follow. An apple strudel-type dessert or chocolate-coated fresh cherries will make a happy end to such a meal.

VEGETABLE SCULPTURES UPON ICE (PAGES 126–7) SHOWING, CLOCKWISE FROM THE TOP: RAW GLOBE ARTICHOKES TOPPED WITH SAFFRON SCENTED CREAMY HORSERADISH AND WALNUT SAUCE, CELERY, DRIED BLACK FUNGUS, RED ONION RINGS, RADISHES, CALABRESE, MANGE-TOUT 'FLOWERS', BABY SWEETCORN, SPRING ONION 'FLOWERS', SHIITAKE MUSHROOMS, COURGETTE 'SPIRALS', THAI 'LONG' BEANS

SPINACH, WALNUT AND CELERIAC LASAGNE

OR MANY years, awkward rectangles of dried lasagne had to be boiled before being combined with the layered ingredients. Now, they can be used straight from the package. This is a light and elegant version of an old favourite. Although I prefer to use plain lasagne, green or egg lasagne can be used, or both, if wished. Select the size of dish which suits the particular geometry of your lasagne, or vice versa.

——— SERVES 4 ———

700 g (1½ lb) young tender spinach, washed
700 g (1½ lb) celeriac, in 1 cm (½ inch) cubes
25 g (1 oz) butter, or 30 ml (2 tbsp) olive oil
salt and pepper
30 ml (2 level tbsp) parsley, chopped
6 sheets of lasagne
350 g (12 oz) cottage cheese

1.25 ml (¼ level tsp) nutmeg, grated
125 g (4 oz) emmenthal cheese, thinly sliced
50 g (2 oz) walnuts, roughly chopped
2 large tomatoes, sliced, halved

GARNISH:
flat leaf parsley

Cook the spinach, torn into moderate pieces, in the water that clings after washing, until brilliant green and barely tender. Drain and press dry.

Cook the celeriac cubes in boiling, salted water in a 1.75 litre (3 pint) shallow flameproof dish for 12–15 minutes or until tender. Drain and mash in the dish with half the butter (or oil). Season well and add the chopped parsley.

Cover with half the lasagne, then the cottage cheese, then the remaining lasagne.

Cover with the spinach and season with the nutmeg, salt and pepper to taste. Arrange the cheese slices along two sides of the dish.

Cook in the oven at 180°C/350°F/Gas Mark 4 for 30 minutes. Sprinkle the walnuts down the centre and dot with the remaining butter. Arrange the tomato slices on either side of the walnuts. Garnish with the parsley and serve hot with crusty granary or French bread.

97

IN THE BACKGROUND, LEFT, GARLANDED PACIFIC POTATO PUREE (PAGE 88)
AND CAMEMBERT IN A NIGHTSHIRT (PAGE 145), AND IN THE FOREGROUND PALETTE OF POTATOES FLAVOURED,
CLOCKWISE FROM THE LEFT, WITH BEETROOT, FAVA BEAN CREAM, PISTACHIO PASTE, FENNEL AND SPRING CABBAGE
AND TAPENARO

JUGGED NOODLES WITH LAZY MAN'S TRUFFLES

R ECENTLY IT occurred to me that provided one contained and covered them well, fine fresh noodles (tagliolini, tagliarini, fresh Oriental egg noodles of various kinds) need not be actually boiled: boiling salted water poured over them for some undisturbed minutes might well do the trick. Meanwhile one could devote those minutes single-mindedly to the sauce with which they would triumph. Large flat black-gilled mushrooms star as my Lazy Man's Truffle: they are almost indecently rich and meaty for a vegetable food. Cooked in butter and milk, then reduced somewhat, sliced up and covered with a scattering of herbs, from humble beginnings there emerges a simple though sumptuous dish.

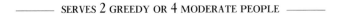

——— SERVES 2 GREEDY OR 4 MODERATE PEOPLE ———

125 g (4 oz) fresh egg noodles
1.7 litres (3 pints) boiling water
30 ml (2 level tbsp) sea salt
450 g (1 lb), or 12 medium flat
  mushrooms, stems removed, caps halved
40 g (1½ oz) butter or olive oil

150 ml (¼ pint) milk (not skimmed)
salt and freshly ground black pepper
2 handfuls of fresh parsley, chervil, chives,
  dill, or lovage
hot crusty wholemeal, granary bread, or
  toasted rolls

Put the noodles with salt into a heat-proof jug, pot or wide-mouthed vacuum flask and pour over the freshly boiled water (preferably kettle-boiled for speed). Stir quickly, cover with cling film or foil, then a weight (or lid) and leave to stand, undisturbed, for 15 minutes.

Heat the butter or oil until melted and bubbling in a large, heavy-based, shallow frying pan and put in the mushrooms, gills downwards, fitting them in so that all the area is neatly covered. Press down using a fish slice or spatula over fierce heat until there is a distinctly mushroomy aroma. (If there is room, add the stems, sliced, or else keep them to flavour another recipe.) Pour over the milk and leave to cook for 1–2 minutes, reducing the heat.

Turn over the mushrooms, re-arranging them as necessary (use tongs or a fish slice) and leave to cook for another few minutes. Reduce the heat but leave uncovered. Continue to cook for another 5–8 minutes by which time the sauce should have grown dark and become creamy-thick. Taste and adjust seasonings.

Test-taste (by bite), and then drain the pasta. If wished, cut the mushrooms with a knife or scissors into quarter pieces in the pan. Shake the pan to prevent the sauce from sticking.

Add the drained pasta to the mushrooms and quickly stir until evenly coated. Serve on crusty or toasted bread, scattered with herbs, scissor-cut or torn.

Do not use very fine 'cellophane' noodles or rice flour noodles (or long rice). Egg noodles, yellowish in colour and narrow in gauge, are what is intended for the 'straw and truffles' effect.

JELLIED MORELS WITH MASCARPONE

I T'S RATHER an eccentricity, this purée, with its jellied topping but it makes a change from the usual mushroom recipe. Make sure your dried mushrooms are aromatic (even dried they should smell very pungent when crushed) and the cheese you choose should be of a mild, creamy type for best results.

Morels appear in the spring or early summer. They are easily distinguished by their brownish, pitted sponge-like caps. The best ones come from France. They can be very gritty so make sure you strain them well.

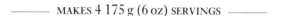

MAKES 4 175 g (6 oz) SERVINGS

50 g (2 oz) dried morels (morilles)
300 ml ($\frac{1}{2}$ pint) boiling water
30 ml (2 tbsp) good red wine
5 ml (1 level tsp) powdered gelatine or
    Agar Agar
25 g (1 oz) roasted cashew nuts, salted,
    chopped
25 g (1 oz) black olives, stoned and
    chopped
125 g (4 oz) Mascarpone or cream cheese

2.5 ml ($\frac{1}{2}$ level tsp) celery salt
2.5 ml ($\frac{1}{2}$ level tsp) mild, sweet paprika
15 ml (1 level tbsp) fresh lovage, borage or
    angelica leaves, torn in pieces

TO DECORATE:
additional lovage, borage or angelica leaves

TO SERVE:
crusty rolls, bread, or melba toasts, warmed

Crumble the mushrooms into a small saucepan of boiling water and leave to stand for 20 minutes, then cook, covered, for 15 minutes.

Stir the red wine into the gelatine and leave to stand until firm. Strain the morels, reserving the liquor, and chop them. If necessary reduce the mushroom liquor to concentrate it. There should be about 150 ml ($\frac{1}{4}$ pint). Stir in the gelatine and heat gently until dissolved. Leave to stand in iced water.

Put the mushrooms, cashew nuts, black olives and mascarpone into a food processor or blender with the celery salt, paprika and torn herbs. Process or blend, minimally, to a chunky state. Remove and gently incorporate half of the slightly-setting gelatine. Smooth the mixture into 4 serving dishes of about 175 g (6 oz) capacity. Put these into the freezer for about 2 minutes or until the surface is firm.

Gently spoon the just-setting gelatine mixture over each pot. Press in additional flourishes of the chosen herb. Chill for a further 45 minutes to 1 hour or leave overnight. Serve in their dishes with crisp-textured bread of some kind.

For those lucky enough to have fresh morels, double the volume and cook gently until tender in a little butter and red wine instead of the method given.

A good Mercurey might not go amiss, and this course could be
followed by a bean salad with almonds, a hot mousse, or syllabub.

HUNTSMAN'S MUSHROOM OMELETTE

THIS IS a no-nonsense omelette served with a bold and unrefined, but tasty, topping, made of dark, meaty, field mushrooms and fresh sage. A 25 cm (10 inch)-diameter frying pan (non-stick is useful) or a heavy well-seasoned large omelette pan, ceramic, and able to be taken to the table) is a particular boon. Only those who have ever discovered ghostly rings of field mushrooms in damp, early morning grass can truly know the pagan pleasure such mushrooms inspire. Our ancestors used wild mushrooms, (high in protein, low in carbohydrates) as a valuable staple food. We should treat them with the respect they deserve (even when they are merely market-purchased) instead of allowing them to be usurped by the ubiquitous pale and perfect button mushrooms.

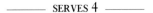

SERVES 4

30 ml (2 tbsp) fruity olive oil
225 g (8 oz) flat mushrooms (preferably wild) quartered
15–25 ml (1–1½ tbsp) freshly squeezed lemon juice
5 ml (1 level tsp) fresh sage leaves, chopped or scissor-snipped

2 shallots, skinned and sliced
8 size 2 eggs
50 g (2 oz) butter
freshly ground sea salt and black pepper

TO SERVE:
fresh thyme sprigs (optional)

Heat the oil in a medium-sized pan and add the mushroom segments, shaking the pan well, for about 3–4 minutes. Add the lemon juice, sage and shallots, and cook gently for about 6–8 minutes, or until the mushrooms are tender and the juices have run freely. Keep aside, over gentle heat.

Lightly beat the eggs with some salt and pepper, using a fork. Heat the omelette pan over fierce heat. Add the butter and tilt the hot frying pan to coat it completely. (The butter must be very hot, almost browned.) Add the eggs all at once, reduce heat, allow to cook, undisturbed, until the base is setting and golden (lift the edges and central bubbles using a blunt knife or spatula, to allow the raw egg to run beneath). Turn up the heat again to brown the base well.

Quickly reheat the mushroom sauce topping.

As soon as the omelette has almost set on top, flip and fold it over (away from the handle is easiest) cut and slide 4 plump segments on to each heated serving plate. Spoon over a little hot sauce on each.

A really fruity Beaujolais or a more hearty Corbières might not be unwelcome and some nutty wholewheat bread, Cheddar cheese and some crisp apples and cobnuts, perhaps, might follow. A leafy salad could precede this country dish.

Pleurottes en Cassoulets

(Little pots of oyster mushrooms)

IN SPITE of being known for their propensity to 'weep' juices when cooked, these delicate mushrooms, becoming more widely available by the day in greengrocers, supermarkets and market stalls, are worth exploring. Although they can be treated in an Oriental way (ginger, garlic, sesame) they are also delicious cooked in a very French way, with lemon and herbs and then given a final grilling with crumbs, in small wide-mouthed pots.

―――― SERVES 4 ――――

75 g (3 oz) butter, softened
2 lemons, freshly shredded zest
1 lemon, freshly squeezed juice
700 g (1½ lb) fresh pleurottes (oyster mushrooms)
60 ml (4 level tbsp) flat leaf parsley, chopped
2 shallots, skinned, thinly sliced
freshly ground black pepper

50 ml (2 fl oz) Muscadet, or other dry white wine
2 1 cm (½ inch)-thick slices of stale wholewheat bread

TO SERVE:
extra flat leaf parsley
lemon slices (see above)

Blend the butter with the zest and juice to a purée, and spread this evenly over the surfaces of the mushrooms.

Put the mushrooms into a large shallow baking dish so that they are not crowded. Scatter over the parsley, shallots and some black pepper. Pour over the wine.

Bake uncovered towards the top of an oven at 180°C/350°F/Gas Mark 4 for 20–25 minutes. Meanwhile preheat the grill until very hot.

Put 4 shallow, but wide-mouthed, dishes or pots under the grill to become hot. Remove the cooked mushrooms from the oven, divide them and their juices between the 4 dishes. Crumble the bread and scatter an even layer over each serving. Grill for a further 2–3 minutes until the crumbs are crunchy and very hot. Transfer the hot cassoulets to serving plates. Put several slices of the remaining lemon, (peel and pith removed first before slicing wafer thin), beside each pot, and an extra sprig of parsley.

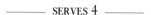

A glass of chilled Muscadet would go down well with this dish, plus some good bread. A salad of watercress, radish and pecan nuts in a creamy dressing, then some strong mountain cheese and fresh seasonal fruits (perhaps figs), would complete a stylish meal.

101

TOURLOU HORIATIKI

(Greek Vegetable Stew)

JUST AS a good many simple classic dishes have practical beginnings, (e.g. bouillabaisse starting from freshly caught mixed fish being tossed into a boiling cauldron of sea water), Tourlou is a vegetable dish (according to Theonie Mark, author of an illuminating book about Greek Island cooking) which begins with a portable clay pot, a little olive oil, seasonings and the produce of the fields into which the family has come to work. Water is usually available on a farm—often, in Greece, it is spring water. A small fire is started, some of the vegetables cook a while in the oil, more vegetables go in, then water and after a time seasonings, garlic (added late to keep its pungency) and a handful of herbs. This dish reminds me of a little of the Tunisian dish, Chakchouka, and of course, ratatouille from France. Clean tastes, pleasant fare.

—— SERVES 4 ——

75 ml (3 fl oz) Greek olive oil
225 g (8 oz) or 1 large, onion, skinned, halved and sliced
275 g (10 oz) aubergines, cut into 2.5 cm (1 inch) slices, halved crossways
275 g (10 oz) or 3 courgettes, cut into 2.5 cm (1 inch) chunks
4 celery stalks, sliced thickly

450 g (1 lb) or 2 large marmande (beefsteak) tomatoes, cut into 1 cm ($\frac{1}{2}$ inch) cubes
150 ml ($\frac{1}{4}$ pint) water
2 garlic cloves, skinned and crushed
5 ml (1 level tsp) salt
freshly ground pepper
2 handfuls of flat leaf parsley

Heat the oil in a medium-sized, flameproof, non-metal pan and sauté the onion and aubergine together for 2 minutes over fierce heat, stirring frequently. Add the courgettes, celery and tomatoes with the water and cover. Reduce the heat and simmer for 25–30 minutes or until the vegetables have amalgamated and formed a sauce. Shake but do not stir them.

Add the garlic and shake to blend it in. Leave uncovered, cook for a further 6–8 minutes, shaking from time to time.

Season to taste. Tear the parsley into small pieces and toss it into the dish. Serve the Tourlou poured over some thick slices of crusty bread if wished, accompanied by some simply cooked macaroni, rice, potatoes or cracked wheat. Serve a resinated wine with this country dish.

A leafy salad, into which cubes of Feta cheese and some black olives have been tossed, could provide an authentic touch. End the meal with some juicy fresh fruit or raisins and some nuts.

METHODIST'S KURMA BRINJAL CURRY

OLD COOKERY books yield many treasures, and reveal the prejudices, predilections and passions of their time. Dishes are often described as 'good-eating'. The ones which state the full particulars of the donors (e.g. c/o Ford Foundation, Kokine Road, Rangoon. Home Address: River Falls, Wisconsin, U.S.A. etc) seem most poignant: whole lives may be glimpsed. Here is a very slightly rearranged version of an English Methodist schoolteacher's curry, from *Rangoon International Cookbook*. In place of the meat I have used aubergines.

—— SERVES 4 ——

125 g (4 oz) fresh 'curds' (made from fresh milk curdled with lime juice), or strained natural yogurt
700 g (1½ lb) aubergines, halved lengthways, cut into 2.5 cm (1 inch) slices
5 ml (1 level tsp) coriander seed
6 green cardamom pods, crushed
5 cm (2 inch) cinnamon stick, broken into pieces
6 whole cloves
5 ml (1 level tsp) white peppercorns (or, if preferred, chilli flesh, chopped)

5 ml (1 level tsp) blue poppy seeds
5 cm (2 inches) fresh ginger root, chopped finely
4 garlic cloves, skinned and chopped
50 g (2 oz) or 1 small onion, skinned, chopped
50 g (2 oz) shelled, blanched almonds
50 g (2 oz), or 1 small, onion
25 g (1 oz) ghee, clarified butter or 30 ml (2 tbsp) peanut oil
freshly chopped mint, coriander leaves or flat leaf parsley

Strain the curds through a jelly bag without pressure. (Alternatively use some thick yogurt or buttermilk, or fromage blanc/fromage frais.)

Put the cut aubergine into a large, shallow, non-metal dish. Grind the curry ingredients (coriander, cardamom pods, including the green pod itself, cinnamon, cloves, peppercorns, poppyseeds, almonds, ginger, garlic) and the chopped onion together.

Mix the resulting curry paste into the drained curds or yogurt and spread over the aubergine. Leave to stand for 30 minutes.

Slice the almonds, if wished. Skin and slice the onion.

Put ghee, clarified butter or oil into an enamelled flameproof saucepan or casserole. Fry the almonds and onion over high heat until golden brown. Drain and keep aside for garnish.

Remove the aubergine pieces from their marinade (scraping the paste off with a spoon, but retaining all of it). Sauté the aubergines over high heat until browned and aromatic. Add the marinade, and enough water (about 150 ml / ¼ pint) to make a good sauce. Cover, reduce heat and simmer for 30–45 minutes, stirring once, or until the aubergines are very tender and 'melting' to the touch. The sauce will be thick and creamy.

103

GREAT GRAINS, RICE AND CEREALS

DEKSHIE FRIED RICE

I N MRS John Barnabas's recipe for Fried Rice (in a 1956 *Woman's Society of Christian Service Cookbook*) the instructions include putting 'the *dekshie* on fire with *ghee* in it.' One assumes that this cooking pan is a wok or some other vessel of that kind. The rice (in her recipe) was soaked for $\frac{1}{2}$ hour before cooking. This is probably because, in countries where rice is a major part of the culture, great variations can be noticed in 'young' (new, moister) rice and 'older' (dry) rice. The soaking makes dry rice quicker to cook. It does, however, also wash away some nutrients, so this practice would not be advisable if rice was one's staple food. Otherwise, apart from some slight changes in order and the equivalent measures, the recipe stands as Mrs Barnabas wrote it 30 years ago. My additional garnishes are optional.

─────── SERVES 4 ───────

50 g (2 oz) ghee or 60 ml (2 fl oz) soya
  oil
100 g (4 oz) or 1 medium onion, skinned
  and chopped
450 g (1 lb) long-grain rice
5 ml (1 level tsp) caraway seeds
6 green cardamom pods, crushed but whole
2 cinnamon sticks, crushed
4–6 cloves

7.5 ml (1½ level tsp) salt
900 ml (1½ pints) water

TO SERVE:
1 ripe avocado, skinned, stoned and sliced
30 ml (2 level tbsp) dried pumpkin, melon
  or alfalfa seeds
1 lemon, cut into 4 or 8 wedges

Put the ghee or oil into a wok or similar pan and heat over fierce heat.
Add the onion and stir until browned. Add the rice and stir until all grains are coated and the rice is golden. Add the remaining ingredients in order, ending with the water.
Cover, (using a piece of foil, if necessary) and reduce the heat to very low. Cook for 20 minutes or until all the liquid is absorbed and the rice is plump. Add the avocado, seeds and lemon wedges, if liked.

Serve with the curry of your choice or with a pea, bean or lentil dish, for maximum nutritional benefit (these are complementary vegetable proteins.)

Arborio Con Zafferano

PROPERLY COOKED, creamy-tender risotto rice is a dish I adore. Arborio rice has an unjustified reputation for being difficult to cook because of the many types and grades available, and the fact that the liquid must be added hot, not cold, and not once, not twice but in 8 or 9 stages during the cooking of a proper risotto. But once you have made this saffron-enriched masterpiece, you will understand why any native of Milan gets sentimental and dreamy when it is even mentioned. Use good ingredients: go to an Italian delicatessen. It is an absolute education and all for free; to me a far more delightful Saturday pastime than polishing the windscreen, the silver, or my infinitives.

—— SERVES 4 ——

1 litre (1¾ pints) vegetable stock, mixed half and half with white wine
75 g (3 oz) butter
15 ml (1 tbsp) pure virgin olive oil
350 g (12 oz) Italian Arborio (medium grain) rice
7.5 cm (3 inch) leek, finely shredded

2.5 ml (½ level tsp) pure saffron strands (or 2 1.25 g sachets of pure, powdered saffron)
7.5 ml (1½ level tsp) sea salt
50 g (2 oz) Parmesan, or Grana cheese, freshly grated
freshly ground black pepper

Have the stock, covered, in a separate pan over low heat ready to add to the risotto once the proper cooking begins.

Heat half of the butter and all of the oil in a heavy-based flameproof casserole, add the leek and stir until it becomes tender but not brown.

Add the rice all at once and stir thoroughly until coated. Sauté for 2–3 minutes, then add 150 ml (¼ pint) of hot stock, stirring firmly and gently as it cooks, until the stock is absorbed, keeping the rice moving constantly so that it does not stick to the pan.

Add a further 150 ml (¼ pint) of stock and continue the steady stirring process.

Continue adding stock and stirring 5 times more. Just before the last addition, add the saffron to the water and wine, so that it will infuse and become hot, ready for incorporating.

Add the saffron-scented liquid, stir until the liquid is half absorbed, then add the rest of the butter (40 g/1½ oz), and half of the cheese. Keep heating and stirring until the rice is creamily bound together, moist, but not wet. Serve with the remaining cheese on top and generous amounts of black pepper.

Serve this noble dish alone, with some good red Italian wine, for example a hearty Chianti Classico, as a companion.

ELEPHANT EAR RICE PACKAGES

THOUGH I may offend some traditionalists and Orientalists by this combination of Indonesian and Thai foods, the pairing seems to work well. Glutinous (sticky) red-black-coloured Thai rice is usually intended for puddings and sweets. If you can locate it (Thai, Oriental and Chinese food specialists stock it) then use it—it is fascinating and gleams like rubies. Otherwise ordinary long-grain rice may be used. I give the Oriental way of cooking rice first, taught to me by a Malaysian college student and colleague: she told me to gauge the depth of water by the length of the first joint of one's index finger. That always seemed to work, but a 2.5 cm (1 inch) measure seems another yardstick which is also foolproof: one frequently quoted by Eastern cooks. Callaloo or Elephant Ear Leaves (from the dasheen plant) are large green edible leaves, often found in ethnic markets and food stalls. Other large flexible and not too tough edible leaves, may be substituted, as wished.

——— SERVES 4 ———

4 large 50 cm (20 inch) Callaloo or
   Elephant Ear Leaves, wetted in water
   and halved

FILLING:
225 g (8 oz) glutinous (black) Thai rice
   or 225 g (8 oz) long-grain (basmati or
   patna) rice
water for washing and cooking rice
salt to taste (optional)
25 g (1 oz) coconut cream block, grated
30 ml (2 level tbsp) coriander leaves

SERUNDENG:
25 g (1 oz) coconut cream (in the block)
175 g (6 oz) desiccated coconut or coconut
   flakes
2.5 ml ($\frac{1}{2}$ level tsp) coriander seeds,
   crushed or ground
2.5 ml ($\frac{1}{2}$ level tsp) cumin seeds, crushed
   or ground
5 ml (1 level tsp) jaggery (see note) or
   dark brown sugar
2 Bombay (small red) onions, or shallots
2 cloves garlic, peeled
1 cm ($\frac{1}{2}$ inch) fresh ginger root, peeled and
   grated
15 ml (1 tbsp) tamarind water (see note)
   or lemon juice
50–75 g (2–3 oz) shelled peanuts

DRESSING:
15 ml (1 tbsp) soy or mushroom sauce
15 ml (1 level tbsp) fresh red or green
   chilli, chopped
15 ml (1 level tbsp) caster sugar
2 garlic cloves, skinned and crushed

SOMTOM SALAD:
350 g (12 oz) raw salad vegetables: choose
   some or all from the following:
   sliced celery sticks, skinned fresh water
   chestnuts, under-ripe pawpaw
   (papaya), green beans (halved), whole
   mange-tout peas (topped), cucumber
   strips, courgette strips
2 large tomatoes, cubed, or cut into 12
   segments
12–16 salad leaves (e.g. pak choy, choy
   sum, kai choy or cos lettuce leaves)

Wipe the leaves, spray or keep damp in water—they become delicate and brittle with drying. To cook the rice in the Oriental way, wash it under running water in a sieve until the water runs clear. Put the rice into a medium-sized, heavy-based lidded saucepan and cover it with cold water to a depth of exactly 2.5 cm (1 inch). Bring rapidly to boiling, cover, reduce to a low heat and simmer, undisturbed, for 10 minutes or until the water is absorbed. (There should be steam holes showing on the top surface.)

Replace the lid tightly, turn the heat to the lowest level, (use an asbestos mat to modify heat if available), and leave to cook for a further 10 minutes, to plump up and dry out the rice even more. (Glutinous rice may need less.)

Leave the rice to cool enough so it may be handled. Taste, and if salt is liked, add some. Grate the coconut cream over and stir through. Add the coriander leaves, chopped or torn.

Halve each large leaf crossways. Divide the rice mixture between the 8 leaf sections and fold up to make neat, regular rectangles or square 'parcels'. Secure each with a wooden cocktail stick or some long tough leaf strips to act as ties. Allow a little room for expansion. Put these parcels to steam in a large wok, (with a rack), or large steamer basket in a saucepan over hot water. (The parcels should not overlap too much.) Steam the parcels while the other ingredients are prepared, about 12–15 minutes.

Blend the coconut, coriander, cumin, sugar, onion, garlic and ginger together with the tamarind liquid, to a paste. Turn into a lightly-oiled pan and stir constantly until the mixture becomes golden brown. Add the peanuts. Spoon into a serving bowl.

To make the salad dressing, mix all the ingredients together. Stir the selection of sliced salad vegetables into the dressing, using the fingers. Pile the dressed vegetables on a platter lined with the whole green leaves. Scatter tomato over all.

Serve the hot, steamed packages, 2 per serving, with some serundeng, and pass the salad for diners to help themselves. The rice packages may be eaten leaf, filling and all (wooden cocktail sticks removed, however).

To make tamarind water, take a cube of tamarind pulp, about half the size of a thumb joint, crush it in 45 ml (3 tbsp) boiling water, then after 5–8 minutes crush, strain and remove solids. If tamarind cannot be located, use lemon juice, lime juice or vinegar. Jaggery is raw lump sugar, generally available in Indian grocery stores.

107

BALANCED BROWN RICE

RICE WHEN served and eaten with peas, beans or lentils is highly nutritious. So, in many parts of the world where rice is an essential staple, such a combination is both commonplace and common sense. It is also wise even in affluent societies, to be resourceful with good ingredients in this way.

These lentils don't need to be pre-soaked, but do make sure you wash and pick them over before cooking. I call this 'Balanced' Brown Rice because the *combination* of rice and pulses results in an improved quota of essential nutrients (eating rice *or* pulses does not).

————— SERVES 4–6 —————

225 g (8 oz) whole, brown lentils
salted boiling water
15 ml (1 tbsp) sunflower, safflower or
   grapeseed oil
225 g (8 oz) long grain brown rice
600 ml (1 pint) boiling water
15 ml (1 level tbsp) sea salt
1 bouquet garni (fresh parsley, bay,
   rosemary and celery)
75 g (3 oz) spring onions, diagonally sliced
50 g (2 oz) walnuts, hazelnuts or
   unblanched almonds, roughly chopped

60 ml (4 level tbsp) low fat natural yogurt
4 fresh tomatoes each cut into 8 or 12
   segments
freshly ground pepper
salt to taste

TO SERVE:
papadoms
spiced tomato sauce

Wash the lentils, discarding any pebbles or debris and put into a medium-sized heavy-based pan. Cover with twice the volume of boiling, unsalted water and cook over moderate heat, partially covered, for 30–35 minutes or until soft but not pulpy. Leave to stand for 5 minutes then drain.

Heat the oil in the emptied, and now dry, pan. Sauté the long grain brown rice until well coated, then add the boiling water, sea salt, and the fresh herb bunch. Bring to boiling point, stir once, cover and reduce heat to a gentle simmer. Leave undisturbed for 45 minutes, by which time all the liquid should have been absorbed.

Remove from heat. Remove the herbs. Add the drained lentils, the spring onions, walnuts, yogurt and tomatoes. Cover and leave to stand for a further 5–8 minutes in a warm place.

Serve moulded, using darioles for variety if liked.

WILD ANNIE'S LAKESIDE RICE

RECENTLY, AMONG the belongings of a young deceased friend, Annie Thwaites, (inveterate traveller, adventurer and diner) was discovered a small pack of what was thought to be seeds, or spices. The carrier bag bore the name of a New York Chinatown supermarket. I realized immediately that here was some very high quality wild rice, silky to touch and pearly dark. I felt I must create some new recipe with this precious bequest since indeed the rice found its way into my kitchen. Annie, I hope, would have approved of this dish. What is fascinating to know is that wild rice is not rice at all but a grass, and it grows best in wet, lakeside habitats. Indians in canoes once used to gather this rare, delicious and expensive foodstuff.

——— SERVES 4 ———

125 g (4 oz) wild rice
450 ml ($\frac{3}{4}$ pint) boiling water plus
  additional 60 ml (4 tbsp) boiling water
5 ml (1 level tsp) sea salt

DRESSING:
50 g (2 oz) shallots, skinned and finely
  sliced
25 g (1 oz) salted butter or 30 ml (2 tbsp)
  pure virgin olive oil

15 g ($\frac{1}{2}$ oz) blue poppy seeds
1 small handful each of fresh chives,
  parsley, chervil, chopped

TO SERVE:
12 quails' eggs, or 8 gulls' eggs, soft boiled,
  in their shells (optional)
12 asparagus spears, cooked and dried
  (optional)

Cover the wild rice with a little cold water. Stir to dislodge any debris, which should float to the surface; discard this. Drain the rice well.

Put into a medium-sized, heavy-based flameproof pan and pour over the first measure of boiling water and add the sea salt. Cover, and simmer gently for 40 minutes or until grains have almost split (sometimes called 'butterflied') and are firm but bite-tender. If after 30 minutes there is no more liquid visible, add the second measure of water. Do not overcook. Drain, return pan to heat, add the finely sliced shallots, butter and poppy seeds. Stir over gentle heat until aromatic. Add the herbs, stir well.

Press into a decorative mould and turn out. Garnish if wished with the eggs, still in their shells, and asparagus, if liked.

Begin with goats' cheese and avocado toasted sandwich portions.
Follow the main course with a vivid, red leafed salad and a good dressing. Round off
the meal with dessert pears and some mellow wine.

BUCKWHEAT FLAT CAKES WITH KASHA 'CAVIAR'

REVITALIZE YOUR pancakes by adding buckwheat flour (also known as blé noir, trigo negro, boek-weit, Saracen corn or sarrasin) for colour, taste and texture interest. Though buckwheat is not strictly a cereal (it looks like tiny beech nuts) it can be treated much like one. Here, a filling of cooked buckwheat (kasha) is served inside the pancakes. Take care not to overcook the kasha—it can become mushy. Yet cooked and seasoned well it is, for me, a veritable vegetable 'caviar'. Fruit vinegar or lemon juice, however, as the final taste enhancer, is essential.

MAKES 16 FLAT CAKES
SERVES 4

FLAT CAKES:
2 large eggs
600 ml (1 pint) milk
30 ml (2 tbsp) olive oil
50 g (2 oz) wholewheat flour
150 g (6 oz) buckwheat flour
30 ml (2 level tbsp) caraway seeds
5 ml (1 level tsp) sea salt

KASHA CAVIAR:
225 g (8 oz) buckwheat (untoasted)
1.4 litres (2½ pints) boiling water
10 ml (2 level tsp) sea salt
25 g (1 oz) dried mushrooms

30 ml (2 tbsp) pure virgin olive oil
30–45 ml (2–3 tbsp) fruit vinegar
2 garlic cloves, skinned and crushed
8–12 trimmed radishes, sliced
freshly ground black pepper

TO SERVE:
60 ml (4 level tbsp) parsley, chives or
*   radishes*
30 ml (2 tbsp) fruit vinegar or freshly
*   squeezed lemon juice (or a lemon,*
*   quartered)*
150 ml (¼ pint) strained yogurt or smetana

Break the eggs into the bowl of a blender or food processor and add the milk and oil. Blend or process for a few seconds. Add the 2 flours, the seeds and salt, and blend or process again, in short bursts, for about 45 seconds. Leave the mixture to stand while the kasha is prepared.

Put the buckwheat into a large, heavy-based, flameproof pan. Toast over high heat until there is a nutty smell and the buckwheat pops and changes colour.

Add half of the boiling water, the crumbled mushrooms and all the salt. Cover, reduce heat and cook gently for 6–8 minutes or until the liquid is absorbed. Add the remaining liquid and cook until fully absorbed and the texture is pleasantly chewy but not mushy, (about 7–8 minutes). Stir in oil, vinegar, garlic, radishes and pepper. Spoon into a serving dish, keep aside.

Pour the flat cake mixture into a jug. Heat a heavy non-stick pan, an omelette pan or a griddle. Brush with a trace of oil. Pour on enough mixture to make a 10 cm (4 inch) flat cake. Cook for 1–2 minutes on each side. Keep cakes hot on a warmed serving dish in the oven, or under a gentle grill.

Add herbs and the second measure of vinegar (or lemon juice) to the kasha, if wished. Encourage diners to spoon yogurt or smetana over each flat cake. Spoon on some kasha caviar, roll or fold it up and eat using the fingers. (If liked, give diners a lemon quarter in place of the vinegar or lemon measure.)

Pinhead Barley with Hazelnut Dressing

T INY, OLD-FASHIONED, 'pinhead' grains of barley are quick to cook and utterly delicious served alone, as a bonus in clear soups, or as part of the 'body' of big, chunky, minestra-type soup-stew dishes. Because pinhead barley is not always easy to locate, (mine came from a small Jewish grocery shop in Soho, near Berwick Street) it pays to buy several pounds at a time for it is good natured, stores well, and always comes in handy. Pinhead oats are more readily available, often in wholefood stores or specialist delicatessen. They, too, are nutty and delicious. The textures respond well to lively dressings, and in this recipe seeds and nuts are the embellishment. If wished, the moist, still-hot mixture can be moulded into shapes to serve amongst salad.

———— SERVES 4 ————

125 g (4 oz) pinhead barley
125 g (4 oz) pinhead oats
boiling water to soften
5 ml (1 level tsp) sea salt
25 g (1 oz) butter
1 cinnamon stick, crushed and broken into
  quarters
450 ml (¾ pint) boiling stock or water

DRESSING:
50 g (2 oz) sunflower seeds
25–50 g (1–2 oz) hazelnuts, roughly
  chopped
60 ml (4 level tbsp) fresh herbs, parsley,
  chives, tarragon, chopped
2 spring onions, sliced
30 ml (2 tbsp) sherry (or wine) vinegar
30 ml (2 tbsp) hazelnut (or other nut) oil

Cover the barley and oats with boiling water and leave to soften for a preliminary 5 minutes. Drain well under running water.

Put into a medium-sized pan with a close-fitting lid and add salt, butter, cinnamon and the boiling stock or a fresh volume of boiling water. Cover and simmer on very low heat for 25 minutes or until grains are plump and tender and most of the liquid is absorbed.

Dry-toast the sunflower seeds and hazelnuts together in a frying pan over steady heat until they darken and become aromatic.

Drain off any excess liquid from the grains (there should not be very much). Stir in the toasted seeds and nuts and the other dressing ingredients. Toss well. Serve hot, warm or chilled as a salad, shaped in 2 or 3 dariole moulds per person, if liked.

*A**ccompany this dish with a cool tomato, egg and cucumber salad, with herbs.*
Fresh fruit ice cream or sorbet, some good hard mountain cheese, cracker biscuits
and some port could make welcome ends to the meal.

111

Maizemeal Polenta Bread
with Pizza Topping

GOLDEN GRANULES of cornmeal, maize meal or polenta originated from a land of gold-worshippers, where it was fortified with lime: a useful trick nutritionally. It travelled to southern Europe and recipes using cornmeal abound—as galettes, cakes, porridge, breads, puddings, pastes. Its golden hue reminds one of sunshine, and the conditions needed for its production. In this recipe the 'bread' can be eaten in segments, plain (with butter or cheese) or it can be topped with strong pizza-type topping for a main course.

——— SERVES 4–6 ———

160 g (5¼ oz) medium or coarse corn, or
   maize meal (sometimes called polenta)
125 g (4 oz) wholemeal (wholewheat)
   flour
10 ml (2 level tsp) baking powder
2.5 ml (½ level tsp) salt
75 g (3 oz) cream cheese
2.25 ml (8 fl oz) milk
1 size 2 egg

TOPPING (optional):
60 ml (4 level tbsp) tomato purée
2 large tomatoes, halved and sliced
25 g (1 oz) dried Italian tomatoes in oil,
   drained, dried and chopped (optional)
2 garlic cloves, skinned and chopped
5 ml (1 level tsp) dried oregano or
   marjoram
12–20 black olives, stoned
50 g (2 oz) freshly grated strong cheese
   (Pecorino, Romano, Cheddar)
50 g (2 oz) soft cheese (Mozzarella,
   Fontina, cream cheese)

Put the cornmeal, flour, baking powder and salt in a mixing bowl. Beat the cheese, milk and egg together and stir into the dry ingredients, mixing to a smooth dough.

Turn the dough out on to a paper-lined baking sheet and pat out into a 25 cm (10 inch) circle. Bake towards top of an oven at 200°C/400°F/Gas Mark 6 for 20–22 minutes or so, or until risen and firm to the touch.

If wished, cover to within 1 cm (½ inch) of the edge with purée, tomato slices, dried chopped tomato, (if used), then garlic, herbs, olives and cheese.

Return to the oven for a further 10–12 minutes or until hot, aromatic and the cheese melted. Serve in large wedges, and accompany with a red and green leaf salad, with a really good dressing.

*T*his dish could be followed by a rice dessert (perhaps with a
fresh fruit coulis) or fresh fruit, then crisp wafers and coffee and, perhaps, grappa,
marc or fruit eau de vie.

Pleasing Peas and Beans

Prayer-Bead Bean Casserole

THIS IS a really straightforward bean dish to leave to cook while you attend to other things. Make sure that the lid of the casserole is close fitting: if not, cover with foil and then the lid. The last minute additions are important and interesting. In summer, this dish is pleasant eaten cool or cold with raw tomato sauce and basil leaves. The black beans used are the glossy, kidney-shaped kind from Venezuela and Brazil, often known locally with affection as 'native caviar'. Chinese black beans are not appropriate.

——— SERVES 4 ———

125 g (4 oz) haricot beans
125 g (4 oz) red kidney beans
125 g (4 oz) black beans
900 ml (1½ pints) stock
2 fresh sprigs rosemary, crushed or 2 fresh
  bay leaves, crushed
1–2 garlic cloves, skinned and crushed

15 cm (6 inch) strip of orange zest
4 cloves
seasoning to taste
30 ml (2 tbsp) tequila or rum

TO SERVE:
natural yogurt (optional)

Check the beans carefully discarding any pebbles or debris. Put the 3 types of bean together in a pan, cover with twice their depth of cold water, bring to the boil, cover, turn off the heat and leave to stand for 1 hour. Drain, discarding the water.

Lightly oil or butter a heatproof casserole or non-metal earthenware lidded pot and add the soaked, drained beans. Add the remaining ingredients including the orange zest studded with cloves, except the seasoning and alcohol. Cover and bake in an oven at 170°C/325°F/Gas Mark 3 for 2½–3 hours or until beans are soft and creamy-textured. Season well and add the liquor. Serve with some cold, fresh yogurt on top, if liked.

Accompany with a soft-textured vegetable such as baked tomatoes and some rice and spinach (either as salad, or as risotto, dressed with a light vinaigrette).

PUREE OF FAVA BEAN

I LIKE TO present high-protein, nutritious purées such as bean purées in an informal context (especially while still warm), with texturally and visually varied accompaniments, such as fruit and vegetable crudités, (minimally prepared). They are also good as appetizers and spreads. Because beans have quite an earthy flavour, I find it useful to add a touch of piquancy with chilli paste (harissa), though a little extra vinegar also does have a similar effect. Make sure you season the purée well or it can turn out rather bland.

——— SERVES 4 ———

200 g (7 oz) Cyprus dried broad or fava beans (skinned variety)
water to cover
1.1 litres (2 pints) boiling water
4 fresh bay leaves, crushed
15–25 ml (1–1½ level tbsp) harissa (or tomato purée)
45 ml (3 tbsp) fruity olive oil

2.5 ml (½ level tsp) Chinese 'taste powder' (see below)
30 ml (2 tbsp) fruit vinegar, i.e. strawberry or raspberry
TO SERVE:
fresh pears, or fennel and celery chunks, crusty wholewheat or granary bread, or herb bread

Put the prepared beans into an enamel or ceramic or other non-metal saucepan (remove any grit). Cover with cold water. Bring slowly to boiling point. Stand for 1 hour.

Drain the beans. Add the boiling water and bay leaves. Cover with lid and simmer until tender enough to fragment easily. Drain. (Reserve the bay leaves and cooking water for a soup recipe, if wished.)

Put the drained beans into a food processor with the harissa, oil and seasoning of choice. Process in short bursts until a fairly smooth creamy purée is obtained. Taste, adjust seasonings, add vinegar. Process, then taste again.

Serve warm, in small pots, or as oval or round scoops, accompanied by the freshly quartered fruits and vegetables and bread for dipping or spreading.

Taste powder: Sharwood's make an interesting condiment of this name, containing a great many interesting tastes. Monosodium glutamate is present but does not predominate. If you dislike even the slightest hint, then use your own home-made citrus seasoning recipe (see page 37).

*P*receded by a clear vegetable soup and followed by a leafy crisp
salad and cheese, this could constitute a balanced meal.
Pass good bread and drink a lusty Barolo or Barbaresco with this dish.

Visible Extras

UCH OF the food in this chapter belongs almost in the 'designer' category: these dishes are intended to woo the diner with their visual inventiveness. Many of them are salads, some are raw. Almost all obey some directive or other: red leaved, green leaved, soft, crisp, warm or mixed in texture. Fruits and vegetables are ideal for making 'food-sculptures' and can be made to dazzle the eye with their virtuosity.

A good part of the pleasure of eating involves the eyes and the food we prepare and present to eat should, as far as possible, delight all our senses. Dining, in a civilized sense, should therefore go far beyond merely satisfying hunger. We should be charmed by the look and feel of food on the tongue, fork and fingers. The texture of food—whether crisp and crunchy or soft and melting—is one of its great joys. Colours should be comely; hues can be selected to complement or contrast with each other, to calm or soothe. It is a good idea, first of all, to follow the guidelines given with each recipe and then develop your own ideas. It is not difficult to be creative, but take care always to prepare the foods so they remain as fresh as possible at eating time.

Visible Extras are enjoyable for more than just effect. This course can become the 'special extra' of the meal—much too charming to miss out. What is more, oddly flavoured or uniquely presented foods (say fresh pineapple with hot pepper, or rosettes of leafy salad with an unusual dressing), can provoke a buzz of excitement, interest, disbelief at your table.

Keeping up appearances (in the culinary sense) is all about knowing when to dare: a geometrical arrangement of sliced tropical fruits upon a stunning lacquer dish or flower-painted antique saladier, with fresh vine leaves looped to the rim can do wonders for the appetite. Be bold, inventive. Use your own instinctive style and Visible Extras will soon become second nature.

TEXTURED, TEMPERATE AND CONTEMPORARY SALADS

SALAD OF RAW TOPINAMBOUR

IF YOU say this recipe name quickly it sounds like childish verse! Topinambour is the French name for knobbly Jerusalem artichoke. Served raw, with a lemony dressing, it becomes delicious and noteworthy. Present it on scoops of radicchio or chicory and decorate the plate with a line or pattern of Citrus, Herb, Nut and Spice Seasoning (see page 37) for real style. Quails' eggs, soft-boiled or pickled (see page 30) could also grace the assemblage.

—— SERVES 4 ——

30 ml (2 tbsp) freshly squeezed lemon juice
60 ml (4 tbsp) sunflower oil
15 ml (1 tbsp) pure virgin olive oil (or hazelnut oil)
225 g (8 oz) Jerusalem artichokes
15 g (½ oz) hazelnuts, roughly chopped

TO SERVE:
8 radicchio leaf 'cups', 8–12 chicory leaf 'cups'
15 ml (1 level tbsp) Citrus, Herb, Nut and Spice Seasoning
optional: quails' eggs, avocados etc.

Mix the juice and the 2 oils together in a non-metallic bowl.

Scrub the artichokes. If a refined result is wished for, pare away the skin. Use a mandoline, food processor, grater or a sharp stainless steel knife to thinly slice or shred them. As soon as each batch is completed, toss it in the dressing.

Divide the slices or shreds between the leaf cups and add nuts. Arrange decoratively at one side of a serving plate. Draw patterns with the seasoning. Serve while the vegetable is beautiful, crisp and fresh.

RED JEWEL-STRAND WINTER SALAD

THIS RED salad contains fruit including gold or red fleshed tamarillos (also called tree tomatoes), sharp vitamin- and mineral-packed fruit of the tomato family. They keep in good condition for weeks in a refrigerator if unbruised and firm when purchased. They are imported from the Pacific and South America. The red-fleshed kind have, to my mind, the most powerful flavour. This salad can be served with warm or cold dressing, as you prefer.

—— SERVES 4 ——

225 g (8 oz) red cabbage, washed, dried
  and chilled
1 head radicchio, chilled
225 g (8 oz) deep red or black grapes
  (Black Hamburg, Chasselas or
  hothouse), halved, seeded
25 g (1 oz) seedless raisins
4 tamarillos or 225 g (8 oz) firm cherry
  or other tomatoes, halved or quartered
1 red onion, skinned, finely sliced

DRESSING:
90 ml (6 tbsp) fruity olive oil
15–30 ml (1–2 tbsp) red wine vinegar or
  balsamic vinegar
15 ml (1 level tbsp) flower-scented honey
freshly ground black pepper
5 ml (1 tsp) soy sauce
5 ml (1 level tsp) Dijon mustard

Using a serrated, sharp stainless steel knife shred the cabbage into fine strands, separating any joined parts (the strands should be finer than 3 mm ($\frac{1}{8}$ inch). Pile into a large glass salad bowl.

Tear the radicchio into bite-sized pieces. Add to the bowl. Add the grapes and raisins. Halve the tamarillos crossways and use a teaspoon to scoop out their dark-red seeded flesh in neat hemispheres (discard the skin). Cut into thin slices and add to the salad bowl. Scatter onion slices over the salad.

Whisk all the dressing ingredients together in a bowl over gentle heat until smooth and barely warm. At serving time add the dressing to the salad and toss well to blend. Serve immediately for crisp results, or, if preferred, allow to stand, in which case the cabbage will soften.

*U*se to accompany Central Course dishes
or as a course on its own.

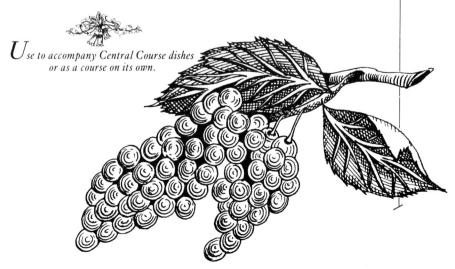

117

EMERALD LEAFY AND CRISP SALAD

(Raw ingredients illustrated opposite page 33)

G REEN SALADS should be treated with respect and care to become the palate-cleansers they were originally intended to be. Use this salad to accompany any Central Course dish (if the wine is really good then substitute red or white wine for the fruit vinegar so as not to compete with its charms) or as a course on its own. Vary the leaves as the season or finances dictate.

Little additions such as soft-boiled quails' eggs, chopped herbed croûtons, flower heads of pansy, nasturtium, white violet or cowslip might be added, for fun, but in this case the salad is no longer strictly a green salad, it is a mixed salad. What matters is the combination of colours, textures, shapes and the feel of the thing under the tongue: there must be balance above all. All the leaves should be chilled before starting.

——— SERVES 4 ———

$\frac{1}{8}$–$\frac{1}{4}$ *head curly endive*
125 g (4 oz) watercress
$\frac{1}{4}$–$\frac{1}{2}$ *head green Batavian endive (escarole, or gross scarole)*
50 g (2 oz) mâche (lamb's lettuce, corn salad)
50 g (2 oz) baby spinach leaves (pousse épinards) (optional)
50 g (2 oz) purslane (optional)
25 g (1 oz) turnip tops, radish tops or beetroot tops
8–12 nasturtium leaves (optional)

1 handful of fresh assorted herbs, to include: chervil, chives, lovage, tansy, sweet cicely, flat leaf parsley, salad burnet, Good King Henry, baby sorrel leaves

DRESSING NOUVELLE:
30–45 ml (2–3 tbsp) raspberry or strawberry vinegar (or wine, as stated)
50 ml (2 fl oz) hazelnut or walnut oil
salt and freshly ground pepper
1 garlic clove, crushed

Depending upon the size and youthfulness of the endives, select about 2 large handfuls of each, including a good section of the central parts. Wash, tear up, or separate leaves into bite-size pieces, easily manageable in size. Wash, shake dry and remove the stalks or bases from the cress and the mâche. Wash and shake dry the spinach, the purslane and the turnip tops. Tear them into small pieces, discarding any tough stems. If nasturtium leaves are small, leave them whole. If large, tear into bite-sized pieces. Use a salad spinner or salad basket to dry the leaves without bruising them. Put into a salad bowl and chill. Scatter herbs, torn or cut, over all.

Make the dressing, shaking the ingredients together in a screw-topped jar, or whisking until emulsified. At serving time pour over and toss until each leaf is gleaming.

RED LEAFED 'DESIGNER' SALAD
(with Dressing Caesura)

THIS *salade rouge* is so attractive that it does really merit the fanciful name. If red-leafed basil is not available, a tiny sprinkling of dried oregano could be used in its place—not at all the same taste, but of similar pungency. When red-leafed basil is available, dry it and store for later use—it is a fascinating salad seasoning. The Caesura Dressing often really does make diners stop and ask for the recipe: it is superb and unusual, yet based on that of the famous Caesar Salad.

SERVES 4–6

3–4 heads radicchio (preferably varying
    from dappled rose to deep crimson)
2 heads treviso
1 small red oak leafed lettuce (feuilles de
    chêne)
2 red-fleshed plums (e.g. Santa Rosa) or
    1 nectarine
2–4 raw baby beets, scrubbed

DRESSING:
2 medium-large eggs at room
    temperature
15 ml (1 level tbsp) rosy mustard (Three
    Fruits Mustard (see page 91))
15 ml (1 tbsp) crème de cassis
45 ml (3 tbsp) hazelnut or walnut oil
30 ml (2 tbsp) red wine vinegar
a handful of red-leafed basil (optional)
sea salt
freshly ground pink peppercorns

119

Wash, dry and chill the leafy salad vegetables. Divide heads of radicchio into separate leaves, halving those which are too large. Mix these in a large salad-serving bowl. Add the treviso, treated in the same manner, and the feuilles de chêne, torn into quarter leaves (but keep inner baby leaves whole).

Remove the flesh from the plums and cut into neat 1 cm ($\frac{1}{2}$ inch) cubes or fine, julienne strips. Cut the beets into 1 cm ($\frac{1}{2}$ inch) cubes. Pile plums and beets in the centre of the salad.

Put the eggs into hand-hot salted water, bring gently back to the boil and simmer for 1 minute. Cover the pan, then remove from heat and leave to stand for 5–6 minutes. The whites will be set but the yolks still liquid. Meanwhile, combine the mustard, crème de cassis, oil, vinegar, red leafed basil and salt and pepper in a screw-topped jar. Shake well.

Scoop the eggs from their shells, mix into the dressing, chopping with a knife until the white is the size of pinenuts and amalgamating the hot, liquid yolk with the other dressing ingredients.

Pour quickly over the prepared salad and take to the table. Toss the salad at table. Serve while the salad is cool and the dressing warm.

If wished, omit the Caesura Dressing and use a normal vinaigrette, or a dressing of 4 parts oil to 1 part red or white wine, with seasonings, if the salad is to accompany another dish and a substantial dressing would be unsuitable.

COMPOTE HOLLIER

WHEN I was very young and my father's garden flourished, I remember a salad which was invariably served on warm Sunday evenings with sliced cold lamb. It included peeled cucumber, sliced tomatoes from the garden (or that of a neighbour) and onion rings, sometimes with herbs, always with pepper and inevitably with vinegar. There was some sugar, I think, to offset the sharpness of home-grown (and somewhat bitter) cucumbers. Here is an elaboration of that theme. It is good served with a risotto or any grain-based dish with some natural nuttiness and chewiness. Buckwheat or wild rice would do nicely. You could replace cucumber half and half with mooli (white radish) for visual interest.

——— SERVES 4 ———

4 large tomatoes
3 large pickled gherkins, (dill pickles) drained
2 ridge cucumbers, (or cucumber and mooli radish)
1 mild onion, skinned and sliced
60 ml (2 fl oz) white wine vinegar
60 ml (2 fl oz) white wine
15 ml (1 level tbsp) honey

5 ml (1 level tsp) green peppercorns, crushed
5 ml (1 level tsp) juniper berries, crushed
15 ml (1 tbsp) salad burnet
3–4 heads fresh lavender, crumbled
freshly ground sea salt
black pepper
15 ml (1 level tbsp) alfalfa seeds

Cut tomatoes, gherkins, cucumber and onion into slices and rings.

Mix the vinegar and wine. Crush the honey, peppercorns and juniper together and blend in the liquids. Pour over the salad in a glass serving dish.

Scatter over torn leaves of salad burnet. Crumble the lavender into little buds and scatter these over the salad. Finish with a diagonal line of alfalfa seeds. Serve within 2 hours.

*S*ome mellow cheese and crisp biscuits then a homemade dessert
such as a trifle or bavaroise might also be welcome.

Geranium and Nasturtium Rice Salad

ONTRARY TO popular opinion, parboiled or 'converted' (a technical term) rice is not merely a convenience food or a sales gimmick. This treatment drives much of the goodness (B vitamins) deeper into the grain itself and therefore, after polishing, (the outer husk's removal) there is more goodness retained by the grain. Rice contains less protein than many other cereals but it is of higher quality. Here it combines with egg and nuts (though peas or beans are the traditional 'complementary' protein foods).

Scented geranium leaves and/or geranium flower water and turmeric root (often available at certain Middle Eastern or Asian supermarkets) give a distinctive touch.

—— SERVES 4 ——

225 g (8 oz) parboiled, 'easy-cook' or 'prefluffed' rice
450 ml (¾ pint) vegetable stock or salted water
8–10 fresh scented geranium (pelargonium) leaves, crushed or 5 ml (1 tsp) geranium flower water
2 fresh bay leaves, crushed
2.5 cm (1 inch) length of fresh turmeric root, shredded or 5 ml (1 tsp) ground turmeric
5 ml (1 level tsp) salt

10 ml (2 level tsp) finely shredded lemon zest
15 ml (1 tbsp) freshly squeezed lemon juice
50 g (2 oz) macadamia nuts (candlenuts) chopped
2 medium-large eggs
1 small head crisp green lettuce (Cos, Webb's Wonder)
freshly ground pepper

TO SERVE:
12 golden nasturtium flowers (optional)

Put the rice, (do not wash or rinse) into a medium-sized lidded pan with the stock or water, crushed geranium leaves, or geranium flower water, bay leaves, turmeric, ginger and salt.

Bring to the boil, reduce to a gentle simmer, cover tightly and cook for 10–12 minutes or until the rice is barely tender and all moisture is absorbed.

Leave to stand, covered, so that grains absorb the full scentedness and become plump. Remove and discard the leaves. Add the salt, zest, juice and chopped nuts. Break the 2 eggs into the hot mixture and stir until well incorporated.

Season, then turn the mixture on to a heated serving dish, surrounding the rice-egg mixture with a garland of shredded lettuce and tucking golden nasturtium flowers amongst it.

*T*his salad would be pleasant after any dry pea-based dish, even a
soup, and could be followed by some good, mature cheese and perhaps some grapes.

PAPAYA MOONS (with pepper mousseline)

THE BRILLIANCE and beauty of pawpaw, a fruit I always associate with my brief visit to Tahiti, always interests me. Its flavour develops in the presence of citrus flavours—in this recipe, limes. (Pawpaws contain papain, a fascinating protein-digesting enzyme, which helps to tenderize meat and fish and poultry—worth remembering for marinades.) The service of this recipe is important: the crescent shapes of red fruit, a spoonful of a mild pepper 'mousseline' or purée (very light) and nuts. Toasted brioche slices and a herb garnish are the final touch.

SERVES 4

1 fresh lime
2 large ripe papayas (pawpaws), thinly peeled

MOUSSELINE:
1 red pepper, opened out flat, peeled, seeds removed, sliced finely
1 small red chilli, seeded
225 g (8 oz) or 1 leek, white part only, shredded
15 ml (1 tbsp) walnut oil

100 g (4 oz) garlic and herbed full fat soft cream cheese
15–30 ml (1–2 tbsp) muscatel or moscat wine (sweet)

TO SERVE:
25 g (1 oz) fresh pecan nuts, shelled (or walnuts)
4 small brioches
fresh herbs of choice

122

Use a zester to remove zest from lime in fine green shreds, then squeeze and extract juice.

Slice the papaya flesh crossways into thin crescents. Discard the seeds. Toss the fruit in the zest and juice to coat completely.

Grill the pepper so that the skin blisters, cooks and can be removed. (This is most easily done by 'charring' the skin then quickly placing the hot pepper in a plastic bag, sealing, then leaving it to stand. The skin loosens and can be stripped off and discarded.)

Sauté the leek shreds in walnut oil until softened. Add the pepper. Fold, (or use blender or food processor), the leek-capsicum mixture into the cheese, adding enough of the sweet wine to make a spooning consistency (it must not flow).

Slice the brioches 4 times lengthways (use the ends for crumbs in another recipe) to make 3 dome-shaped slices per serving. Toast these 12 little 'toasts' and serve them hot, with a pile of the papaya 'moons' at their centre, a spoonful of mousseline and the pecan nuts beside. Add a herb garnish of choice.

This course would be delicious accompanied by some more chilled moscat (or muscatel) wine; a rice, noodle, bulgur or potato dish of some kind as well, and a crisp green salad. Good cheese and dried muscatels or raisins could round off this meal.

RONDES VERTES

(Leek salad)

HERE IS a lively dish using leeks, those endlessly amenable vegetables. It has an Oriental taste yet a certain Mediterranean vividness: the leeks should retain their brilliance, curved shapes and a degree of bite.

Wasabi is very pungent and has a slightly different flavour to the usual western horseradish. It is generally only available in Japanese shops or in specialist oriental delicatessens. If it is unavailable you can substitute ordinary horseradish though the flavour won't be quite the same.

—— SERVES 4 ——

1.4 kg (3 lb) medium to large leeks
boiling salted water or stock
15 ml (1 level tbsp) wasabi (green Japanese horseradish powder)
15 ml (1 level tbsp) green herb mustard or Dijon mustard
30 ml (2 tbsp) rice vinegar (mirin) or sherry vinegar

50 ml (2 fl oz) green olive oil
150 ml (5 fl oz) cows' or sheeps' milk yogurt
sea salt
freshly ground pepper
45 ml (3 level tbsp) flat leaf parsley

Trim off and discard the roots and tough discoloured dark green ends of the leeks. (These can be used in soup).

Cut the leeks evenly into 5 cm (2 inch) lengths. Wash the pieces quickly in warm water.

Steam-boil the leeks in 1 cm ($\frac{1}{2}$ inch) of boiling water or stock in a large, tightly lidded saucepan, shaking the pan occasionally, until bite-tender but not soft, (about 6–7 minutes). Drain, (reserving stock, if wished for stock or soup). Return leeks to pan, cover.

Stir, shake or blend the wasabi, mustard, vinegar, oil and yogurt together until creamy. Taste and season. Serve the leek piled up in a dish with rivulets of dressing spooned over. Scatter with parsley sprigs.

*S*erve this dish hot or warm with Sushi (see page 22) or a rice
dish of some other kind then follow it by good cheese (perhaps a goat cheese) and
scented fresh fruits in syrup, or grappa.

123

Insalata Asparagi Del Duca

T HAT RARE commodity, Italian balsamic vinegar, (aceto balsamico) is often called *aceto del duca* in deference to the dukes of Modena, home of this wonderful condiment. It is deep, rich, strong and long-matured. I buy mine in Fauchon, the mecca for food-lovers in the Madeleine, in Paris, because it is still difficult to find in London. Recently my local delicatessen, Mr Christian, near the Portobello Road market, began to stock it, in eccentrically-shaped small flasks. Hopefully balsamic vinegar will soon become easy to locate in all good specialist food stores.

In this simple salad, barely cooked, diagonally-cut asparagus is dressed and served, still warm or just cool, in this vinegar, with some superlative Italian olive oil (*olio extra vergine de oliva*) added for absolute perfection. (If the asparagus is really young sprue (fine 'wild asparagus') it could be served raw, with such a dressing.)

——— SERVES 4 ———

*350 g (12 oz) bunch of young, straight-
    tipped green asparagus*
salted water
*thinly sliced wholemeal or granary bread
    and butter curls*

*60 ml (4 tbsp) Italian pure virgin olive
    oil*
15 ml (1 tbsp) aceto balsamico
freshly ground black pepper

Using a rolling motion, roll-cut the washed asparagus spears (leaving off the lowest 2.5 cm (1 inch)) into 2.5 cm (1 inch) chunks, moving the stems as you cut, to give the required diagonal surfaced effect. (Using a sharp stainless steel knife—any real resistance to the knife means the asparagus is tough, so keep these portions for soup or a green mayonnaise.) Leave tips whole and perfect.

Wait until your guests are seated and hungry. Pass some wafer-thin unbuttered brown bread and some good butter curls. Place asparagus in a steamer or basket or colander over boiling salted water and cook until barely tender or 'al dente' (this will vary considerably, according to quality and youthfulness, and also to personal preference).

Remove the vegetables to a hot serving dish. Just before serving, (for the best colour), pour over the oil and the vinegar, season and then toss gently using the fingers. Serve warm. If the asparagus must be cooked ahead, cool, but do not chill it. Dress it at the table.

Ideally, perfect green asparagus spears are straight tipped, (not curved), and the mauve-tinted budding 'scales' should not have become too coarse or flower-like, for this means the best moments are gone. Neither should there be any ridges or striations in the green flesh: it should feel tender to the touch, yet firm and crisp, not floppy nor flaccid. Stand spears upright in some iced water in a cool place, or in a refrigerator and use without delay if possible. Natural sweetness deteriorates rapidly and so does flavour. At the greengrocer's, if the asparagus bases look pale, blanched and woody, take it as a sure sign that you should buy, instead, some baby leeks. Use the very same dressing. Your guests will not complain.

HOT CUCUMBER CURACAO

A CHARMINGLY SIMPLE cucumber and orange dish, thickened with pale golden cornmeal (maize meal) or semolina, which gives a curious roughness to the sauce. The Curaçao could be replaced by another citrus liqueur if wished, but its effect is important and interesting. Do not omit the final flourish of fresh herbs.

Serve the dish as a hot salad, alone, before or after a cereal course of some kind, while tastes and colours are at their best.

———— SERVES 4 ————

700 g (1½ lb) or 2 large cucumbers
50 g (2 oz) salted butter
30 ml (2 level tbsp) cornmeal (or semolina)
150 ml (¼ pint) freshly squeezed orange juice
salt

freshly ground pepper
10–15 ml (2–3 level tsp) freshly shredded orange zest
30 ml (2 tbsp) Curaçao
1 handful of fresh lovage, borage or mint, shredded

Skin the cucumbers thinly. Halve them lengthways and use a teaspoon to scrape out the seeds to make 4 'boats'. Cut crossways into 2.5 cm (1 inch) chunks.

Gently fry the cucumbers in butter in a large shallow pan until they are greenish-gold but not soft. Push the cucumbers to one side of the pan, sprinkle in the cornmeal or semolina and stir over gentle heat for 1–2 minutes.

Add the freshly squeezed orange juice, stir, and season to taste. When the sauce has thickened, (this takes about 3 minutes) shake the pan to coat the cucumber. Add zest, liqueur and fresh herbs, shaking the pan a little.

A fruity, fragrant white wine would not be unwelcome with this dish. After this, a leafy salad, some blue cheese and some fruits, (such as bananas or passion fruit), could taste pleasing.

125

VEGETABLE SCULPTURES UPON ICE

(Illustrated opposite page 96)

THIS IS a centrepiece for a party or special celebration. Vegetables of your choice, selected for freshness, beauty, colour and crisp tenderness, are well washed and drained, cut in various ways and then packed on crushed (or cracked) ice. Tools which are useful are a zester and canelle knife, combined, a spiral cutting tool, (recently marketed as one of a 3-tool set), a sharp, stainless steel paring knife, and a stainless steel serrated knife. A bowl of iced water on hand is also essential. Dried Chinese cloud ear mushrooms are available from Chinese supermarkets, while Japanese shiitakes are now beginning to appear in larger city supermarkets.

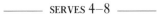

———— SERVES 4–8 ————

2 large, perfect, raw globe artichokes (with mauve tips, if possible)
1 lemon, halved
6–8 baby green courgettes
4 baby yellow or black courgettes
50 g (2 oz) dried cloud ear mushrooms or black fungus
boiling water
125 g (4 oz) fresh Japanese shiitake (matsutake) mushrooms
225 g (8 oz) baby sweetcorn on the cob
2 bunches of scarlet radishes with tops and roots
225 g (8 oz) baby mange-tout peas
75 g (3 oz) spring onions, trimmed
125 g (4 oz) calabrese (purple sprouting broccoli)
225 g (8 oz) Thai 'long beans' (optional)

225 g (8 oz) yellow pattypan squashes
1 head celery (with green leaves)
1 red onion, skinned
125 g (4 oz) hop shoots
12 20 cm (8 inch)-lengths of fresh chives
225 g (8 oz) enoki mushrooms

SAUCE:
150 ml (¼ pint) whipping cream or fromage blanc battu
30 ml (2 level tbsp) grated horseradish
25 g (1 oz) walnuts, chopped (or ground almonds if preferred)
1.25 mg (or 1 sachet) powdered saffron
30 ml (2 tbsp) freshly squeezed lime or lemon juice

Remove the stalks and halve the artichokes lengthways. Pull out and discard the inner leaves and fluffy 'choke' portion, using a teaspoon or curved-bladed knife. Rub cut surfaces with a cut lemon. Place the artichokes at the top centre of a layer of crushed ice, facing out like flowers in 4 directions.

Top and tail the green courgettes. Halve crossways then use the spiral cutter to form them into spirals. Put decoratively on the ice, pulling the tendrils out. Use the canelle knife to make cross-hatched areas, rather like a Dufy or Matisse drawing, on both sides of the other courgettes. Halve each if wished. Place on ice.

Steep the cloud ear mushrooms in some boiling water, covered, for 8–10 minutes. Leave to stand.

Meanwhile, score criss-cross slashes across the top of the shiitake (matsutake) mushroom caps, if they are big enough. Otherwise, leave as they are. Trim stalks a little. Halve or quarter if large. Place on the ice with the baby sweetcorn, left whole.

Pull off and discard any yellowed leaves from the radishes. If wished cut canelles (channels) in them in the sign of an asterisk, or else use a knife to remove small circles, leaving them polka-dotted. Place on ice, in bundles, leaves facing outwards.

Cut 7 or 8 parallel slashes from the tip end half way down towards the stem of each mange-tout. Submerge in iced water and leave to curl outwards like fans. Give the same treatment to the spring onions, at both ends, making 7 or 8 intersecting slashes each time. Submerge these, too, in iced water.

Halve the broccoli and calabrese lengthways if large, otherwise divide into smaller florets and leave whole. Stack these decoratively on the ice.

Top and tail the long beans (these should be about 50 cm (20 inches) long. Wrap these around each other to make bracelets. Arrange upon the ice.

Cross cut the pattypans downwards in a series of parallel lines, at right angles, and leave submerged in the iced water. They should open up a little.

Cut the celery into 5 cm (2 inch) diagonal pieces, but leave small inner leafy portions whole. Arrange on the ice.

Slice the red onion finely, then separate carefully into single rings. Arrange upon the ice.

Arrange the hop shoots in 8 or 12 tiny bundles using chives to tie them up, knotting them or making bows.

Drain the re-hydrated mushrooms, remove all vegetables from the iced water and arrange, in their categories, upon the ice. Scatter the tiny enoki mushrooms prettily among the other vegetables. The ice should now be covered fairly evenly.

Whip the cream until soft peaks form or stir the fromage blanc battu. Fold in the horseradish, nuts and saffron. Spoon some neatly into each of the 4 artichoke 'cups'. Take to the table amidst sustained applause.

*H*ave some hot bread on hand, large napkins and a fragrant
Touraine wine, such as a Vouvray, a Montlouis or a San Gimignano.

PINEAPPLE ACAPULCO

DURING OUR voyage to Europe, some years ago now, our ship stopped at Acapulco. The pure colours, staggering heat, barefoot petticoated peasant girls, the decorated wares and the tortillas were not the only things I took in, open-mouthed. A child tugged at my skirt offering me fresh pineapple. She carried cayenne in a twisted cone of paper. She sprinkled it over the cut fruit, laughing at my surprised face. The fruit tasted delicious and I have been a convert ever since. The tequila is optional, but interesting—a wonderful taste-awakener at the end of a summery, or ethnic-style meal, or at any time. It occurs to me that the continental habit of grinding black pepper over wild or mountain strawberries is not so unlike the Acapulco tradition.

——— SERVES 4 ———

*1 large, fresh, scented pineapple with
  perfect green leaves*

*60 ml (4 tbsp) tequila (optional)
2.5 ml (½ level tsp) cayenne pepper*

Remove the base so that the pineapple will stand evenly. Slice off the leafy green leaves, on a tiny section of flesh, reserving 12 or so of the best ones.

Using a very sharp serrated stainless steel knife, slice downwards to remove the outer skin of the fruit, but not so far that you remove the 'eyes' (which constitute, to me, perfectly acceptable dietary fibre, and good exercise for healthy jaws! The polka-dot pattern always makes me think of plantations and sunny hillsides.)

Halve the fruit down the centre. Cutting with a sawing motion, (always at 45° angles), reduce each pineapple half to 9 or so wedges.

Pile 4 or 5 wedges upon each chilled serving plate. Sprinkle with the tequila.

Arrange 3 pretty leaves to one side of each serving. Sprinkle a little red hot pepper along one leaf. Encourage diners to dip the fruit into the cayenne as they eat it, using fork or fingers.

MOSAIC OF SPICED SOLSTICE FRUITS (PAGE 136)—A DESSERT, PRESERVE, SALAD
AND DECORATION ALL IN ONE

PAWPAWS STUFFED WITH KIWI FRUIT

I FEEL SOMEWHAT defensive about kiwi fruit (known originally as Chinese gooseberries). The tender, never tough-centred New Zealand-grown variety are so superior to those of most other nationalities—yet the public frequently does not appreciate the difference, so inferior fruit often sells for a similar price. Look for plump, egg-shaped, never-wrinkled fruits, with a velvety, golden, teddy-bear skin. You will not be disappointed. In this recipe, kiwi fruit and liqueur (astringency and sweetness) with the additional touch of pepperiness to develop the effect seem rather curious contradictions, but they do augment the effect of the pawpaw. Not an inexpensive dish, this, but well worth trying when good fruit is available.

———— SERVES 4 ————

2 ripe, orange-speckled, soft-to-the-touch
* pawpaws (papayas)*
60 ml (4 tbsp) Aurum (or other citrus-
* flavoured) liqueur*

4 kiwi fruits
freshly ground black pepper

Smell the pawpaws. They should be scented. Slice them in half lengthways using a stainless steel knife. Scoop out and discard the seeds and central pith.

Pour a tablespoonful of liqueur into each fruit.

Slice off and discard the ends of the kiwi fruit. Use a vegetable peeler to remove the brown hairy skins so that little is lost. Halve the fruits lengthways then cut each half into 4 long segments. Tumble 8 segments attractively in the cavity of each pawpaw. Serve immediately, or chill a little if preferred, then grind a fine sprinkling of black pepper over each just before serving. (It acts as an aromatic, and is surprisingly pleasant.)

*S*erve this decorative salad after some hot dish, having prepared it
and chilled it some time in advance, for simplicity's sake. Follow it with a green leafy
salad and finally cheese.

PEACH SORBET BELLISSIMO (PAGE 155); IN THE GREEN GLASS, ADRIAN'S
ALMOND SWEETMEATS (PAGE 144) AND APRICAROSSET (PAGE 150); IN THE FOREGROUND, BERRIES IN THE SNOW (PAGE
153) AND EDWARDIAN LOVAGE SYLLABUB (PAGE 151)

129

Anise-Scented Chestnuts with Spiced Spinach

FRESH CHESTNUTS, which are often rather trying to skin and prepare, become easy to handle when treated by the following method. They absorb scent from star anise heads which are also exceedingly decorative in the final arrangement. The spinach is minimally cooked, so it remains brilliantly green and its unusual rather Indian-inspired spicing will surprise many guests. A pleasant new way of serving two old favourites. You will find fresh and dried lemon grass in oriental food shops (some supermarkets also now stock fresh lemon grass). If it is not available, substitute a strip of lemon peel.

—— SERVES 4 ——

700 g (1½ lb) chestnuts in the shell
10–15 heads of star anise, roughly crushed
5 ml (1 tsp) rose or citrus flower water
1 cinnamon stick, crushed
1 head lemon grass, slit lengthways (optional)
400 ml (¾ pint) vegetable stock (see pages 44–45)
1.4 kg (3 lb) leaf spinach (redroot, branching type or spinach beet or spinach), washed

water
50 g (2 oz) ghee or butter (or 60 ml (4 tbsp) mustard or peanut oil)
15 ml (1 level tbsp) coriander seeds, crushed
2.5 ml (½ level tsp) cayenne pepper
1.25 ml (¼ level tsp) ground asafoetida powder
2.5 ml (½ level tsp) nigella seeds (optional)
salt (to taste)

Slash each chestnut deeply through the shell and flesh, almost halving it. Put into a saucepan with the star anise, rose water, cinnamon stick, lemon grass and stock. Cover closely, bring to a lively boil, reduce heat and leave to simmer for 45–60 minutes, or until much of the liquid is absorbed and the chestnuts have softened enough to crush easily. Twist them apart into halves, keep warm, with a little of the reserved aromatic liquid.

About 10 minutes before the estimated end of chestnut cooking time, put the washed spinach (and the water that clings to the leaves, adding 45 ml (3 tbsp) water or vegetable stock) into a heavy-based, covered pan and cook over moderate heat, shaking the pan from time to time, until it is tender yet still brilliant green, and about half the original volume (4–5 minutes). (If this volume of spinach is cooked longer it will dwindle to quarter volume and lose its brilliance.)

Tip the spinach into a colander and drain well. Add the ghee, butter or oil to the dry, still-hot pan and sprinkle over the coriander, cayenne, asafoetida powder and nigella seeds. Add spinach and toss until the leaves gleam and aromatic smells prevail. Heap the spinach and surround it with the chestnut halves, still in their shells, the star anise heads and a trickle of liquid. (The chestnuts are removed from the shells using a fork, and eaten with a mouthful of green leaves.)

Cured, Pickled and Preserved Garnishes

IDDEN AWAY within many of the good meals I have eaten in my life have been certain small extras—a little pot of hot condiment, a bowl of delicate pickles, a jar of gleaming fruits packed in syrup or alcohol. A platter of tiny sweetmeats might appear with coffee, or a goblet of sugar-cured foods covered by a crust of spiced sugar to accompany a rather simple dish. Every culture has some of these gems: from a handful of carefully applied herbs to salty seeds, or crumbled seaweed preserves. Apicius-style honey-and-wine fruits have ancient origins in first century Rome, yet their charm persists to this very day.

From a red basil mustard to a Moorish-style marinade, from mosaic-style fruit layers to Bacchus-invoking grape clusters, in a perfect ruby syrup, here they are! Recipes like these cannot help but supply a personal note to the foods you present. Small portions, judiciously used with other foods, can invigorate a jaded palate and revive flagging interest as well as bringing smiles to the faces around your table. They can also encapsulate the smells and sensations of another season long after it has gone. They remain in the mind's eye, the tongue's memory long after the meal has ended and been forgotten.

Because they were adjuncts, not main dishes, I often forgot to ask about and record the recipes. This is a pity because many of these 'cured' (and I use the word in the widest sense) garnishes are absolute treasures. They can make bread and cheese into a banquet, revitalize a plain risotto. A kind of alchemy is at work—these garnishes are natural stimuli for the eye, the tongue and the imagination, to be used with discretion.

HOMEMADE RED BASIL MUSTARD

I F YOU grow basil, particularly beautiful red basil, or can locate it via an informed herb supplier, use it in this delicious hot and concentrated condiment. Use a small dab of it with creamy cheese or stir it into dressings, sauces or marinades. It is also delicious (though powerfully hot) used on its own as an appetite-awakener, with other bland foods.

——— MAKES 1 SMALL POT, ABOUT 90 g ($3\frac{1}{2}$ oz) ———

5 cm (2 inch)-strip of dried orange peel, crumbled (or the peel of 1 orange, fresh)
5 cm (2 inch)-strip of dried lemon peel, crumbled (or the peel of 1 lemon, fresh)
30 ml (2 level tbsp) dried (red) basil flowers (or 60 ml (4 level tbsp) fresh red basil flowers)
25 g (1 oz) black mustard seeds
25 g (1 oz) white mustard seeds

5 ml (1 level tsp) Polyglot Hot Seasoning (see page 38) or pink peppercorns
5 ml (1 level tsp) sea salt
15 ml (1 level tbsp) honey
10 ml (2 level tsp) mild, sweet paprika
2.5 ml ($\frac{1}{2}$ level tsp) turmeric
15 ml (1 tbsp) extra virgin olive oil
30–45 ml (2–3 tbsp) white wine vinegar

First, if no dried peel or flowers are available, dry some by putting in a low oven (140°C/275°F/Gas Mark 1) overnight, or for some hours. Thread the peel portions onto wooden skewers.

Separate the basil flowers into little buds (the stems removed) then lay them out on a baking tray with baking parchment (on a level below the peel), to dry. When this process is complete, store these aromatics in dry, clean, opaque glass, or china jars or pots, with screw top lids.

Using half of the given dried quantities, grind, pound or crush the peel and flowers with the 2 mustard seeds, the pepper and the sea salt, to a powder. Turn into a bowl. Repeat the process with remaining half.

GARLIC HEAD PRESERVE

O NCE IN a Persian restaurant in Bayswater, intrigued as I was by watching the flat bread being made, and baked in a tandoor-type oven, I also noticed jars of preserved garlic on a shelf. The proprietor withdrew a whole head, put it on a plate, arranged some torn bread, soft white cheese and cucumber pieces nearby and sat down to chat with his drinking companions. This is my version of a garlic preserve, very pungent (it is particularly good after long storage), it is not unlike miniature pickled onions, and is well worth the small effort. It also looks very decorative.

—— MAKES 1 LARGE JAR ——

8–10 whole bulbs of garlic (pink or purple
    skinned for preference)
600 ml (1 pint) white wine vinegar
10 juniper berries
10 cloves

20 black peppercorns
1 sprig (3 or 4) fresh bay leaves, crushed
50 g (2 oz) Greek Hymettus honey
1 sachet ground saffron or 1.25 ml ($\frac{1}{4}$ tsp)
    strands

Using a long, sterile needle (such as a darning needle), pierce the bulbs of garlic in 20 or 30 places (depending upon garlic size), so that the marinade can penetrate. Pack the garlic upright in a sterile jar into which they just fit, but try to avoid bruising the flesh.

Bring the vinegar and the 4 aromatics to the boil, then pour over the garlic, inserting the bay sprig down one side of the jar. (The liquid should completely cover the garlic. If necessary, top up with a little extra vinegar, brought to boiling point.)

Spoon over the honey. Allow to cool. Cover with a non-metal, screw-top lid and invert several times to blend.

*S tore in a cool, dark place. Use the garlic to flavour bland foods,
to eat with cheese and brown bread, or to slice (skin removed, of course) into salad for
added piquancy. The liquid can be used, sparingly, as part of a vinaigrette.*

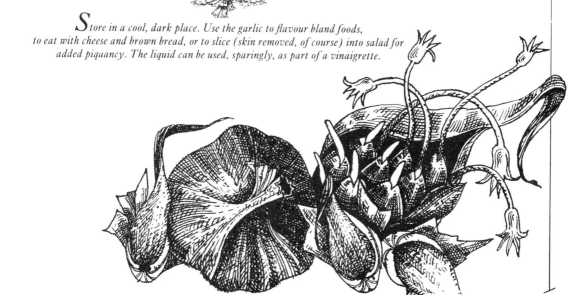

BACCHANALIAN GRAPE PRESERVE

(Illustrated facing page 128)

I F WE could invite the great god Bacchus down from his classical pediment I feel certain he would soon reach, with avid pleasure, for deserved refreshment. The plump, individually studded grapes of this preserve, (complete with stems and all)— would intrigue such a creature, I am sure. So would the potent red liquor surrounding them. Make this beautiful preserve only when you find tight, perfect fists of grapes. They must be black—dark, dry and with their original bloom.

——— MAKES 1.5 litres (2¾ pints) ———

*1 large or 2 small tightly-packed bunches
   of black grapes (e.g. Ben Hannah)
   weighing 550 g (1¼ lb) approximately
100–110 cloves
2 vanilla pods, split lengthways*

*6 dried lime leaves
300 ml (½ pint) hot water
225 g (8 oz) caster sugar
225 ml (8 fl oz) dry white wine
450 ml (¾ pint) vodka*

Put a clean, dry, 1.5 litre (2¾ pint) preserving jar on an oven tray in a 200°C/400°F/Gas Mark 6 oven and leave it to sterilize. Carefully working up from the tip of the bunch, stud each grape with one clove.

In a medium sized, lidded saucepan, heat the vanilla pods and lime leaves with the hot water. Add the sugar, heat until dissolved and bring to boiling point. Remove from the heat, cool a little, then add wine and cover so that the alcohol does not evaporate.

Insert the grapes into the hot sterilized jar, pushing carefully so that they fit. Pour over the hot syrup. Return the jar to the oven. Leave for a further 30 minutes. Meanwhile sterilize the rubber seals in boiling water. Remove the jar and top up to overflowing with the liquor. Carefully apply the rubber seal, close and secure the jar. Stand in a draught-free place until cool then store in a cool, dark, dry place. Leave for at least 1 week, but up to several months (if curiosity allows) before opening. The colour will have deepened to a rosy bacchanalian glow.

Once the jar is broached it is no longer sterile, so store it in the refrigerator.

PUMPKIN PRESERVE KHALOUL

THE FIRST time I ever tasted pumpkin preserve in syrup was while working on the hugely successful Robert Carrier partworks—the recipe was unlikely, I thought. Since my role as a food stylist was to prepare then arrange it, photogenically, before the camera, it was not my part to question why. We tasted it—delicious, though rather sweet. Here is an evolved Ferguson version, but be warned: it is still very scented but sweet. One should use it sparingly, with some sharp-flavoured natural yogurt or soft acidic cheese, like Feta.

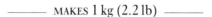

MAKES 1 kg (2.2 lb)

900 g (2 lb) even-shaped pumpkin slices
450 g (1 lb) preserving sugar
300 ml (½ pint) boiling water
2 cinnamon sticks, crushed

50 cm (20 inch)-length or orange,
*   clementine or mandarine peel*
1 lemon, juice

Remove the skin from pumpkin using a paring knife or floating-blade peeler. Scrape out the thread-like filaments from the centre. Discard (or keep and dry) the seeds. Slice the section crossways into 2.5 cm (1 inch) thick curves.

Pour the boiling water over the sugar, cinnamon and orange peel in a large, heavy-based, lidded pan. Stir, over gentle heat until completely dissolved. Add the pumpkin slices, arranged in a jigsaw pattern, in one layer and bring to boiling once again. Reduce to a gentle simmer. Cook for 35–40 minutes or until the pumpkin has become dark and rather translucent, turning the pieces in the syrup so that they cook very evenly on all sides.

Carefully remove the pumpkin to a hot, sterilized jar, using sterilized tongs. Add the lemon juice to the syrup in the saucepan and rapidly boil for 3–4 minutes. Pour the thick, boiling syrup over the slices, using gentle pressure, if necessary, to make sure they are all submerged. Allow to cool, cover and store in the refrigerator.

Carefully treated, the pumpkin pieces should keep their shapes. Even if they break a little, they are delicious, though they look most fascinating when complete, so it is worth a little care and effort.

This is a short-to-medium term preserve (it may be used straight away or over a period of say, 2 weeks). Serve as a dessert with some of its syrup and sharp yogurt or Feta, or with rice, legumes, curries or wheat-based dishes as a 'sambal' or seasoning.

Mosaic of Spiced Solstice Fruits

(Illustrated facing page 128)

T HE HANDSOME straight-sided jar containing this extraordinary fruit sculpture invention looked so curious that I kept returning to the refrigerator hour by hour to see if I had imagined its fascination. The fascination remained, though the layers of sugar had vanished and were slowly dissolving into syrup. They left behind them a perfect dappled mosaic of foods, not at all unlike the constructions I have visited in the past at Carthage, Delos and Rome. It is pleasing to make and fun to eat. It is dessert, preserve, salad and decoration all at once—wonderful for special occasions. The drained fruit, a little of the syrup and a few of the seeds are eaten. Have a number of friends to help celebrate this special dish—one which I created almost by accident—when you have access to wonderful (preferably unsprayed) fresh fruits: high summer and Christmas both often provide the impetus (hence its name, solstice).

——— SERVES 8–12 ———

35 ml (7 level tsp) dried orange flower
   petals
25 g (1 oz) coriander seeds
25 g (1 oz) black mustard seeds
25 g (1 oz) fennel seeds
225 g (8 oz) caster sugar
225 g (8 oz) fresh dates, halved lengthways
   and pitted

275 g (10 oz) or 4 fresh carambola (star
   fruit) halved crossways
225 g (8 oz) or 4 fresh figs, topped and
   quartered lengthways
275 g (10 oz) or 2 Temple or blood oranges
275 g (10 oz) portion of 'sugar baby'
   watermelon, derinded and cut into
   2.5 cm (1 inch) cubes
275 g (10 oz) or 4 large limes

Into the base of a large, dry straight-sided 1.5 litre (2¾ pint) glass jar, (with non-metal top or ground glass stopper), sprinkle 5 ml (1 level tsp) of orange petals. Cover with dates, press down firmly. Sprinkle over 30 ml (2 level tbsp) sugar and 5 ml (1 level tsp) each of the 3 seeds. Sprinkle over another 5 ml (1 level tsp) of orange petals.

Arrange the carambola with star-edges outwards to form the next layer. Sprinkle, as before, with the same amounts of sugar and the 3 seeds, then the measure of orange petals once again.

Arrange a layer of figs, pink flesh outwards. Sprinkle as before. Remove the zest and pith from the Temples. Quarter the fruit and arrange a layer. Sprinkle as before. Layer the cubed watermelon next. Sprinkle as before.

Remove zest and pith from the limes. Halve the fruit crossways and arrange a layer. Use firm pressure to push the fruits down. Complete the layers using all remaining sugar, seeds and petals. The fruit and spiced sugar should fill the jar completely.

Wrap cling film round the lid or stopper and press downwards, or screw into place.

Chill for at least 1 day and up to 1 week, or until the sugar completely forms a syrup and the fruit becomes aromatic yet not discoloured. (A crust of sugar may, however, remain on top which is perfectly acceptable.)

Serve, straight from the chilled jar, at the table, for all to see, with some accompanying tart-flavoured crème fraîche or soured cream, if wished as a dessert, or to accompany a really stylish cheese platter.

If other fruits must be substituted then try to start with firm, dense, dark-fleshed fruits at the base and finish with limes. Fruits with decorative forms are those you must choose, with juiciness, colour and distinct tastes. Orange scented petals are often available at good herbalists, homeopathic pharmacies, and wholefood stores.

MAGIC SEA LETTUCE GARNISH

D O YOU remember those children's playthings which, when put into a bowl of water, magically blossom into a garden? This recipe is virtually the same: purchased dried laitue de mer, (sea lettuce) when covered in sea salt crystals and boiling water at the table, transforms itself into brilliant green tissue and gives off a wonderful aroma of the sea. All that remains to be done is to drain it, toss it in aromatic dressing and serve it, either alone, or as a taste-teaser, or as the garnish for noodles or rice. It is enchanting. (If dried sea lettuce is not available, the recipe works to some extent using Japanese dried seaweed shreds, and even sheets of Nori from wholefood and Oriental foodstores, but the effect is undramatic, and the tastes only fair.)

137

——— SERVES 2, 3 OR 4 ———

15 g ($\frac{1}{2}$ oz) dried sea lettuce (laitue de mer)
15 g (1 level tbsp) sea salt crystals and boiling water
10 ml (2 tsp) sesame oil (light or dark)

15 ml (1 tbsp) mirin, (Chinese rice wine), Muscadet, or dry sherry
pinch chilli powder or other seasoning of choice

Because this is so much fun to watch, take the crumbled, black, dried sea vegetable to the table in a heatproof glass vessel, bowl, jug or large goblet. Scatter over the salt. Pour over some boiling water and watch. Stir a little—the sea vegetable blossoms green!

Once you and your companions have exhausted the pleasure of watching this phenomenon, or in about 5 minutes, drain and remove the sea vegetable to a flat dish. Toss with the remaining ingredients and offer diners chopsticks, satay sticks or tiny forks to help themselves.

Alternatively, toss the dressing on top of some freshly cooked noodles (Japanese soba noodles, or cellophane noodles, perhaps) or rice and stir it in as a taste-garnish.

Sea lettuce (*ulva lactuca*) is a green algae, and looks like lettuce. It is also known as green laver. It is not to be confused with dulse.

TINDORI AND BAIE ROSE PICKLE

TINDORIS (or tindis) are exquisite vegetables, often found in Asian supermarkets and now in certain large supermarket chains, which look and taste like miniature, tender-fleshed cucumbers but with pale orange or scarlet centres. The flesh is firm, delicate and crisp. Fanned out (after a series of parallel lengthways slashes) they resemble exotic blooms. Baies roses (pink peppercorns) from the Reunion Islands are brilliant and aromatic peppercorns, now available in small jars. The preserving medium here is acidulated water (using glacial acetic acid, see note below) and honeyed syrup with some chillies for pungency. This is a medium-term preserve, but unlike pickled onions and dill pickles the tindoors soften with time, rather than staying crisp. If crispness is desired, make and eat this preserve within 1 week (it is good even after 2 days) after which time they will soften and mellow considerably.

———— MAKES 1 litre (1¾ pints) ————

450 g (1 lb) young, even sized tindori
350 ml (12 fl oz) boiling water
125 g (4 oz) pure honey
15 ml (1 tbsp) glacial acetic acid

30 ml (2 level tbsp) baies roses (pink
peppercorns) or black peppercorns
2 tiny red chillis, slashed lengthways twice

Top and tail each wiped tindoor—it will stand up easily for slash-cutting. Carefully slash each one 4 times, almost to the base, so that the 'petals' fan out. Position in a 1 litre (1¾ pint) sterilized preserving jar. Continue until all are used. The tindori should almost fill the jar.

Bring the water and honey to the boil, leave to cool slightly, then add the acetic acid. Add the peppercorns, and the 2 red chillies. Cool quickly over ice.

Pour the liquid over the tindori in their jar. Allow to stand for 1 hour to completely cool, then cover with non-metal lid or screw-top non-metal seal. Store in the refrigerator and leave for at least 1 week, although they taste delicious well before this time.

Glacial acetic acid is available from chemists. Treat it with respect and keep it out of the way of young children, tightly sealed. To dilute glacial acetic acid to the equivalent of vinegar, use 1 part to 20 parts water (i.e. 15 ml (1 level tbsp) to 300 ml (½ pint) water). One bottle will last indefinitely.

Happy
Endings

T O END the perfect meal, or round off an everyday repast well, takes some thought and planning. Too often good, but weary cooks are tempted to reach for the ice cream (synthetically coloured and flavoured), purchased cakes or oversweet biscuits of doubtful freshness or horrific expense. Wiser cooks will use good fromage blanc or yogurt, with a quickly dressed raw fruit, or fling a home-made syrup over some seasonal berries.

This chapter provides some lovely, sensible and straightforward recipes with which to complete a family meal, a coffee afternoon, a late supper party or a visit from old friends. Quickly assembled, startlingly original and sumptuous, these final offerings will grace any table. From Greek shortbreads to sorbets and granitas, from jellied mousses to a pastry-wrapped whole Camembert, from splendid syllabubs with herbs to whole stuffed flowers—here is a chance to end with as much panache as you began. Many of these recipes can be partly or fully prepared some time ahead, for relaxed entertaining, and effortless family meals.

Balance is the key. Follow light food with a sweet course more substantial; clear the palate of spicy flavours by an iced or chilled fruit concoction. Mildness often seems apt after strong tastes; dairy products or cheese should never occur within the same meal more than once. With opulent desserts serve but a little portion. Cold puddings often seem satisfying after a series of hot dishes. With delicate new textures and culinary experiences (let us say, fresh blooms stuffed with a sweet mousse) go gently—serve only one per diner.

If in doubt go for 'true dessert'—really good fruit of optimum temperature (sometimes this means chilled, sometimes at sunny room temperature) and perfect, ripe cheese. Nuts can be splendid, cracked open at the table.

A tisane or a cup of coffee, a digestif and a sweetmeat and the party is over.

FIGS IN SYRAH SYRUP

LUSCIOUS SYRAH grapes with their berry-like scent are now established world-wide, (often known as Shiraz, Sirac, Serine), and the wines made from them have become important and praiseworthy. To make a syrup from them seems unspeakable—but it works, especially when used with fruit such as figs. Enjoy the remaining wine with the cheese course preceding this dessert. Make sure the figs you buy are ripe (but not overripe) or they will lack flavour.

—— SERVES 4 ——

25 g (1 oz) caster sugar
10 ml (2 level tsp) lemon zest, freshly shredded or grated
15 ml (1 level tbsp) orange zest, freshly shredded or grated

2.5 ml (½ tsp) citrus flower water
125 ml (4 fl oz) Syrah wine
8 or 450 g (1 lb) fresh black or green figs

TO SERVE:
fig, vine or other edible leaves

Stir the sugar, scented water and a little of the wine in a pan over gentle heat until dissolved. Add the zest, and the remaining wine. Halve or quarter the figs lengthways, arrange prettily on a stemmed compotier, glass stand or glass bowl and pour over the syrup.

Leave for 20–30 minutes (although this dish can be used almost immediately, or stand for some hours).

If Syrah wine is not available, use another fragrant red. I have even used Pineau de Charentes, or scented white wine with fair results.

I myself like this best when fairly freshly made, allowing just enough time for flavours to relate. Tuck some leaves into one side of the stand or bowl.

140

DORMOUSE AND TEAPOT TART

L ONG BEFORE I ever read about it, the Dormouse in the Teapot Salon de Thé in the Marais area of Paris had attracted my interest and I had taken tea there with great amusement. I tasted a citrus-frangipane type of tart, fresh from the kitchen in a generous wedge, and relaxed with cups of their excellent tea. The waiters are as charming as the habitués are varied. It is worth a visit but my spicier and simplified version of this tarte au citron is also good for stay-at-homes who fall asleep over the teapot.

SERVES 4–6

75 g (3 oz) unsalted butter, cubed
150 g (5 oz) unbleached white flour
40 g (1½ oz) molasses sugar
5 ml (1 level tsp) ground cinnamon
1.25 ml (¼ level tsp) ground nutmeg
1 size 2 egg yolk
10 ml (2 tsp) light, golden or dark rum

FILLING:
1 size 2 egg white
2 size 2 eggs
3 size 2 egg yolks

1 lemon, shredded zest, freshly squeezed juice
2 limes, shredded zest, freshly squeezed juice
5 ml (1 tsp) orange flower water
175 g (6 oz) or 150 ml (¼ pint) fromage blanc battu
50 g (2 oz) icing sugar

TO SERVE:
Rum-flavoured fromage blanc battu (optional)

Process the butter, flour, molasses sugar and spices together in short bursts until mixture resembles coarse breadcrumbs. Add the egg yolk and rum and process in 1 or 2 bursts (the fewer the better) until the mixture forms a ball with hand pressure. Wrap in cling film and chill for 30 minutes.

Flatten the pastry ball and then using finger and knuckle pressure, push and shape the pastry so that it covers the sides and base of a 20 cm (8 inch)-diameter metal flan ring, placed on foil. Remove the flan ring on to a preheated baking sheet. Prick all over using a fork, cover the base with more foil and stand a 15 cm (6 inch)-diameter plate or dish in the centre as a weight.

Bake 'blind' at 190°C/375°F/Gas Mark 5 for 15 minutes. Remove the plate or dish and foil and leave to dry out in the oven for 3–4 minutes. Stand the pastry case in a larger baking dish (to prevent spillage while cooking).

Whisk the egg white, eggs and yolks together. Add the zests, juices, citrus flower water and fromage blanc battu and the icing sugar, stirring to blend.

Pour this filling into the hot pastry shell and bake at 200°C/400°F/Gas Mark 6 for 10 minutes then reduce heat to 180°C/350°F/Gas Mark 4 for a further 25–30 minutes or until just set but not yet shrinking from the edges.

*S*erve warm in little wedges, with the rum-flavoured fromage blanc battu, if liked, or serve it very cold.

ISNEAUVILLE CALVADOS AND APPLE SORBET

RECENTLY, IN a country inn not far from Rouen, in a little town called Isneauville, dear friends Isabelle and Jean-Michel initiated us into some of their local culinary delights. We sat in a pretty, charming room and looked out of the window at the church, which appears to be in the middle of the road. In these parts a *trou Normand* of Calvados (this literally makes a 'hole' to make a welcome way for another course, and acts as a palate-tingler) is not uncommon. But this country establishment used lovely Normandy apples in the guise of a stunning sorbet. This recipe causes that pleasant evening to return to my mind each time I taste it, and I long to return for another visit, before the inn, its chef and the quiet little town become too well known by other than locals.

MAKES 1 litre (1¾ pints)

SERVES 4–6

*450 g (1 lb) flavourful green eating apples
   (not red-skinned)*
*300 ml (½ pint) apple juice (preferably
   made using a 'juicer')*

100 g (4 oz) caster sugar
60 ml (4 tbsp) Calvados
*4 apple leaves (or 4 'corkscrews' of green
   apple skin) to garnish*

Quarter, core, then quarter again but do not peel the apples. Put these with a dash of the apple juice into a non-metal saucepan and cook, covered, until the apple is tender and barely pulpy, about 3–4½ minutes, depending upon apple size. Stir in the sugar.

Reduce to a purée using a blender or food processor. Cool over ice. Stir in the remaining juice and the Calvados.

Pour into a freeze-proof 1 litre (1¾ pint) plastic, lidded container and fast-freeze for 2½–3 hours, stirring twice, first after the first 1½ hours, (when crystals have formed around the edges), then again 1 hour later. Stand in a refrigerator for 20 minutes to 'season' before whisking, beating or stirring to a grainy cream.

Serve in scoops on chilled dishes, in chilled stemmed goblets, or in purchased coupelles (tulip-shaped crisp wafer biscuits) with a garnish of an apple leaf or a curl of peel.

If you own a sorbetière then follow the manufacturer's instructions.

GREEN-PINE SHERBERT CHARTREUSE

SHERBET, SORBET, water ice or granita—there's not a lot to separate them, except for language, ice crystal size, amount of sugar and whether or not an egg white has been added. Here we have another success story of savoury and sweet working well together: pineapple frozen with a peppering of fresh clean leaves of cress as part of the mixture. The liquor addition is good, too. Chartreuse, whether green or yellow, adds a scented, aromatic tang to this frozen confection.

——— SERVES 4 ———

350 g (12 oz) caster sugar
225 ml (8 fl oz) dry white wine
3 limes, freshly shredded zest and squeezed juice
75 g (3 oz) bunch watercress, washed, coarsely chopped

450–550 g (1–1¼ lb) fresh pineapple, cut into 1 cm (½ inch) chunks
30 ml (2 tbsp) yellow or green Chartreuse

TO SERVE:
4 stems of perfect watercress

Stir the sugar and wine together in a pan over gentle heat until the sugar is dissolved, then cool over ice. Stir in the lime zest and juice.

Put the chopped watercress into a food processor with the pineapple. Process in short bursts until blended to a speckly rough purée. Add the sugar syrup and blend again.

Stir in the liqueur and turn the mixture into a shallow, freezeproof plastic lidded container.

Cover and fast-freeze for 2½–3 hours, stirring from sides to centre after 1½, 2 and 2½ hours. (If a sorbetière is available, follow the manufacturer's instructions.)

Remove from freezer. Stir, (use an electric beater on slow speed, or a food processor), until a crumbly texture results. Serve in piles or scoops in chilled goblets or on chilled glass dishes, with a few watercress leaves.

A 1.1–1.4 kg (2½–3 lb) whole pineapple will yield the required amount of flesh for this recipe.

ADRIAN'S ALMOND SWEETMEATS

(Illustrated opposite page 129)

LAST NOVEMBER, Adrian Bartlett, an established artist and friend, invited me to his British Council exhibition in Athens. I went, and it was a huge success. What is more, the tourists had left. The Athenians themselves had the sleek air of content that comes with calm, normality and the onset of a new season. The days were clear, sea and sky an astonishing blue, and the quiet walks I took through and around the Acropolis yielded many new treasures. The sweet-sellers' trolleys, at Monastirion, were a delightful kaleidoscope of yellows, greens, pearly whites and tawny browns—nuts, seeds, mastic, nougat. Coconut ice, rolled in spiced coconut, took bizarre forms. Marzipan I also saw later presented in an altogether new way. I walked, nibbled, and reflected that in each place one goes there is always room for discovery. Here is one of the creations inspired by that memorable, late autumn trip.

———— MAKES 400 g (14 oz) OR 40–50 pieces ————

275 g (10 oz) ground almonds
1.25 ml ($\frac{1}{4}$ tsp) rose water, citrus flower
   water or fruit eau de vie
225 g (8 oz) granulated sugar
125 ml (4 fl oz) boiling water
1 orange, finely shredded zest

TO DECORATE:
75 g (3 oz) shelled pistachio nuts, roughly
   chopped
25 g (1 oz) icing sugar for dusting

Put 225 g (8 oz) ground almonds into the bowl of a food processor with the flavouring.

Place the sugar and boiling water in a large saucepan and bring to the boil stirring to dissolve any sugar on the sides of the pan. Reduce heat and cook at a steady bubble for 10–15 minutes or until the syrup reaches the soft ball stage (a sugar thermometer registers 240°F). Remove from heat.

Pour the hot syrup down the feed tube of the food processor and process until the mixture reaches a cohesive paste, which happens almost immediately. Remove the still-warm paste from the processor and knead into it the 50 g (2 oz) ground almonds and the zest, working quickly on a clean dry surface. (A marble slab is excellent.)

Pat out the paste to a long rectangular shape, about 1 cm ($\frac{1}{2}$ inch) thick. Halve crossways, then cover one surface with nuts. Make a sandwich with the top layer. Press down and pat out once more to 1–2 cm ($\frac{1}{2}$–$\frac{3}{4}$ inch) thick.

Using a cleaver or long straight knife, cut the marzipan and nut sweetmeat into tiny diamonds or fingers. Alternatively, use a cutter to cut ovals, or decorative shapes of your choice. Dust with icing sugar, place in an airtight box or container, separating the layers with bakewell paper (or sweet papers) and store in a cool dark place.

*S*erve these, with a hot, black coffee, a glass of iced water and
maybe a tiny glass of ouzo or Metaxa brandy, at the end of a meal, in place of
dessert, or, as the Greeks do, when unexpected friends call in.

144

CAMEMBERT IN A NIGHTSHIRT

(Illustrated facing page 97)

EVER SINCE I learned some camembert 'lore' from my Norwegian-French friend, Bille, I have enjoyed the particular qualities of this famous and sometimes now undervalued cheese. She told me that if you are buying a packaged camembert, always look for a wooden (not plastic) box and waxed paper (not plastic) wrappings. She also taught me how to judge when camembert is at its best and what the smell should be like, (never ammoniac), and that slightly young, Normandy Camembert fermier, is really delectable. Here is a recipe that suits any camembert, even the rather timid supermarket variety.

—— SERVES 4 ——

1 10 cm (4 inch) diameter camembert, chilled
50 g (2 oz) unsalted butter, melted
5 ml (1 level tsp) grated nutmeg
15 ml (1 level tbsp) molasses sugar

4 sheets filo pastry (about 45 × 30 cm/ 18 × 12 inches)

TO SERVE:
damson or plum preserve

Unwrap and chill the cheese. Have the oven heated to 230°C/450°F/Gas Mark 8, with one rack positioned fairly near to the top.

Stir the melted butter, nutmeg and sugar together, then brush the mixture quickly over one side of each of the filo pastry sheets.

Criss-cross the filo sheets one over the other on a baking sheet. Place the cheese in the centre. Carefully pull up the pastry points, (or shirt tails), towards the centre, twist and pinch loosely to secure, pulling out the 'frills' prettily. Bake for 15–18 minutes or until the pastry is gold-tinged and crisp.

Serve hot, in segments, with a spoonful of damson or plum preserve. Have some good French bread to hand, and some good red wine, perhaps a Touraine Gamay, a Brouilly or even a Juliénas.

145

CHOCOLATE ARABICA SORBET

VOLUPTUOUS DELIGHT: an unashamedly grainy chocolate and coffee flavoured sorbet. It is a treat to be enjoyed on special occasions—neither one's palate nor one's waistline should be assaulted by such concoctions too often. But like all good things it should be appreciated for its own particular merits.

Arabica coffee, which is the finest quality, is indigenous to Ethiopia where it can be found growing wild at high altitudes.

MAKES 1 litre (1¾ pints)
SERVES 6–8

200 g (7 oz) unsweetened (bitter) chocolate
450 ml (¾ pint) hot, freshly made espresso coffee (arabica for preference)

150 g (5 oz) caster sugar
15 ml (1 tbsp) dark rum

Break, chop or crush the bitter chocolate into a bain-marie, or a large bowl over hot water. After a few minutes, add the hot coffee, the sugar, and the rum. Stir until dissolved. Remove the bowl and cool quickly over ice, stirring constantly.

Pour into a freeze-proof plastic, lidded container (1 litre (1¾ pint) capacity) and fast-freeze for 3½–5 hours, stirring after the first 1½ hours or when crystals have formed around the edges. Continue to stir at hourly intervals.

Remove from the freezer. Stand for a few minutes in a refrigerator to 'season' before serving in scoops on chilled dishes or stemmed glasses, or in hollowed-out orange skins, with a garnish of citrus leaves and flowers.

If you own a sorbetière, then follow the manufacturer's instructions for sorbets; the texture will be not quite the same as with this method, however.

GREEK SHORTBREAD 'MOONS'

THESE ARE some of the most delightful celebration biscuits I have ever tasted. When I first went to Greece, the old, white, icing-sugar dusted tins at the back of the coffee shops always intrigued me. The brittle, plump, horseshoe (or moon-shaped) biscuits which tasted so superlative, retrieved like treasures out of their white-coated hideaway, had a special secret charm. Many cooks have told me their versions: they are as varied as the colour of the Aegean. Finally, after much advice and experiment, I have decided that Greek or Cypriot dry-roasted unsalted almonds, unblanched, give by far the best results. This recipe is from Greece with love!

MAKES APPROXIMATELY 24

225 g (8 oz) butter, at room temperature,
   cubed
50 g (2 oz) caster sugar
1 size 2 egg yolk
30 ml (2 tbsp) Ouzo or Metaxa brandy
125 g (4 oz) unblanched, roasted almonds
50 g (2 oz) cornflour

275 g (10 oz) all purpose white flour
120 ml (8 tbsp) rose or citrus flower water
   (or a mixture of both)
225 g ($\frac{1}{2}$ lb) icing sugar
extra icing sugar (as required for dusting
   and storing)
rice paper, bakewell paper or cellophane

Soften the butter in a warmed bowl, then whisk until light and fluffy. Add the sugar, yolk and liquor of your choice. Continue whisking until very pale.

Grind, process, or coarsely chop the crisp-textured almonds. (Do not over-process, they should be quite rough, grainy and coarse.) Add the nuts and both flours to the creamed mixture. Blend until smooth.

Cut the mixture into quarters, then divide each quarter into 7 or 8 pieces to make 28–32 walnut-sized pieces. Roll these into neat balls, then push a floured index finger into each, pushing from the opposite direction with the opposite palm, to form crescents. Arrange evenly over 2 bakewell paper covered oven sheets.

Bake at 180°C/350°F/Gas Mark 4 for 45 minutes. The biscuits should dry and become firm with no sign of browning whatsoever on the bases.

Turn off the oven and leave the biscuits until almost completely cooled. Put the flavouring into a cup and quickly immerse each biscuit. (Alternatively use a brush to paint the flavouring over each biscuit, but the first method is quickest and most effective, although it requires a deft touch.)

Have the icing sugar in 2 smallish, but deep bowls. Drop each wet, freshly dipped biscuit into one containing icing sugar then lift out and turn (in one gentle movement) to coat the other side, in the second bowl. (The icing sugar must adhere all over completely, thickly, like a white veil. No surface of biscuit should show—merely dusty whiteness, so handling must be careful.) Allow icing sugar to stick and coat. Put the biscuits into a large rice paper- or bakewell paper-lined tin or biscuit jar, sprinkling extra icing sugar first over the base and then over each layer. Put a layer of paper between each. (The biscuits should never touch.) When this ritual is completed, seal and store in a cool dark place and produce for any and all festive or happy occasions.

OLD-FASHIONED NUT PRALINE

CARAMELIZED SUGAR (or toffee) is exciting to make but it becomes very hot, so be careful with it. Glucose syrup (useful in the making of icings and confectionery) is available from chemists. If the weather is cold, it may need to be softened first, as described below. Use traditional almonds or the more old fashioned continental choice of pistachio nuts if you prefer for this dark, flavourful praline, useful for so many culinary purposes.

———— MAKES ABOUT 400 g (14 oz) ————

125–175 g (4–6 oz) shelled almond, pistachio or cashew nuts
50 g (2 oz) glucose syrup
250 g (9 oz) granulated sugar

50 ml (2 fl oz) water
5 ml (1 tsp) white wine, or strawberry or tarragon vinegar

Spread the nuts evenly on an oiled sandwich tin.

Put the container of glucose syrup into hot water for $\frac{1}{2}$–2 minutes, or until soft enough to measure. Place on the scales and remove 50 g (2 oz) to a 2.3 litre (4 pint) heavy-based saucepan.

Add the sugar, water and vinegar and cook, uncovered, over moderately high heat for 8–10 minutes, stirring until the sugar has completely dissolved.

Bring to the boil without stirring, and cook for a further 6–8 minutes, tilting the pan as the toffee browns. Keep a watchful eye—when it darkens and smells of caramel and temperature has very nearly reached 350°F (caramel stage), pour over the nuts.

When the praline is quite cold, crush between layers of greaseproof paper using a rolling pin. Store in an airtight jar.

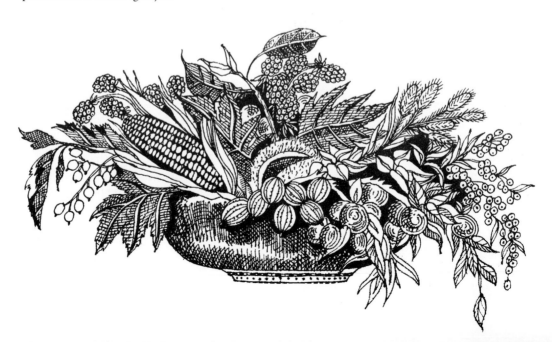

Praline-Stuffed Floral Salad

I F YOU have green fingers then the ideal blooms for this dish are Day Lilies, (famous, edible, non-irritant yellow lilies, much used in the Orient, where they are known, dried, as Golden Needles). As the name suggests, their delicacy makes them difficult to market; scented roses are an alternative, as are courgette flowers or nasturtiums. The praline may contain almonds or other nuts (see opposite) such as pistachios for example. Praline can be made well ahead, but stuff and decorate the flowers no more than 1 hour before the meal, if possible. Add the liqueur or Dressing Nouvelle at the very last moment and dress each serving with edible green leaves of your choice. A fascinating combination.

—— SERVES 4 ——

8 small or 4 large scented roses (or flowers of your choice)
225 g (8 oz) fromage blanc
2.5 cm (1 inch) fresh root ginger, peeled and grated finely
2 size 2 egg whites
pinch salt
45 ml (3 level tbsp) caster sugar

90 ml (6 level tbsp) powdered or crushed praline
60 ml (4 tbsp) Aurum or Galliano liqueur or 60 ml (4 tbsp) Dressing Nouvelle (see page 118)
50–75 g (2–3 oz) tender, edible, green leaves such as nasturtium, mâche, dandelion etc

149

Check roses for cleanliness. Open the petals if necessary and remove the central portion if wished. Gently blend the fromage blanc with the grated ginger.

Whisk the egg whites with the salt until soft peaks form. Add the sugar by degrees, whisking until stiff peaks form. Fold the cheese into the egg white.

Stand each flower in a champagne flute (or an egg cup, if necessary) to make the handling easier. Scatter some praline inside each flower. Using a teaspoon, gently prise apart the petals (if necessary). Insert the mousse mixture by the spoonful, until the flowers are evenly filled. Scatter the remaining praline over each.

Serve the flowers upon a pool of liqueur or Dressing Nouvelle.

These eccentricities could be used as a dessert, as a starter, or as a palate-reviver between courses. Select the savoury or sweet dressing according to use.

APRICAROSSET

(Illustrated opposite page 129)

HAROSSET, A Jewish Passover recipe combines here very satisfactorily with a sweetmeat of my mother's which uses dried apricots, a whole orange (zest, pith and flesh) and other aromatics. It is easy to make, delicious and valuable to keep on hand for unexpected visitors and quick desserts.

———— MAKES 50–60 SWEETMEATS ————

225 g (8 oz) sultanas
225 g (8 oz) dried dates, pitted and chopped
75 g (3 oz) shelled walnuts or pecan nuts, chopped
125 g (4 oz) unsulphured, dark dried apricots, chopped
125 g (4 oz) brightly coloured sun-dried apricots, chopped

1 seedless orange, chopped into 1 cm ($\frac{1}{2}$ inch) cubes
5 ml (1 tsp) citrus flower water
15–30 ml (1–2 tbsp) Kummel or Aquavit (optional)
125 g (4 oz) sesame seeds, toasted

Put all the ingredients except the sesame seeds into a food processor. Process in short bursts, stirring and pushing down from the sides occasionally, until a stiff, even-textured paste is obtained. Do not overprocess. Some texture is pleasant and the mixture may become too soft.

Divide into 50–60 small marble-sized balls, clenching in the hands tightly to compact the mixture firmly. Roll in the toasted seeds. Store the balls in petit-fours cases in layers in a large airtight jar, box or tin, divided by layers of card, cellophane or bakewell paper. They look decorative, rather curious and interesting.

Serve chilled in place of dessert, with liqueurs, with coffee, or at room temperature for morning tea or afternoon coffee accompaniments.

EDWARDIAN LOVAGE SYLLABUB

(Illustrated opposite page 129)

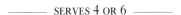

THIS FROTH of a dish could be equally well used as the start to a meal as well as to the ending of it. Lovage, a delicious green celery-like herb, often grows wild, and once it is established in a garden, it is tenacious. It can work well in cocktails and also in soups. Here it is in an ambiguous role — but the taste is memorable. Mint can be used instead, but it does give a completely different effect.

——— SERVES 4 OR 6 ———

75 ml (3 fl oz) dry white wine
30 ml (2 tbsp) freshly squeezed lemon juice
15 ml (1 level tbsp) freshly shredded lemon zest
40 g (1½ oz) caster sugar
150 ml (¼ pint) double cream, chilled
25 g (1 oz) fresh lovage or mint leaves

TO DECORATE:
fresh roses and rose petals, violets or violas, or pansies (optional)

Mix the wine, lemon juice, zest and caster sugar and leave to blend for 2 hours until the sugar has softened then stir well. Add the chilled cream and whisk vigorously until the mixture is light, frothy, forms soft peaks and is very thick.

Chop, shred or purée the lovage and fold it through the mixture quickly. Spoon into goblets and serve with French bread or melba toast, tuiles, langues de chat or crêpes dentelles can be served if the syllabub is used as a sweet course. To go really over the top, serve upon a pedestal dish smoothed into a mound, scatter with fresh rose petals, 1 or 2 whole rose blooms (and leaves) and a few violas, pansies or violets, for Edwardian charm. Present this fragrant green construction surrounded by its Edwardian bouquet or garland.

The syllabub itself is good-natured and can be made half a day in advance, but decorations should be added just before serving time.

KERRITANGI DESSERT

THIS TEN-MINUTE dessert is an adaptation of a rich pie recipe told to me by my friend and assistant Kerry, after her recent trip to the Pacific. The original, rather over-opulent recipe has a pastry base, then a layer of caramel before the fruit and its flavoured cream. This version omits some of the labour and many of the calories yet retains great charm and sumptuous flavours and textures.

——— SERVES 4 ———

6 large firm bananas
60 ml (4 tbsp) citrus liqueur such as
    Aurum, Triple Sec or Mandarine
5 ml (1 level tsp) freshly shredded lime
    zest
15 ml (1 tbsp) freshly squeezed lime juice
15 g ($\frac{1}{2}$ oz) molasses sugar
150 ml ($\frac{1}{4}$ pint) whipping cream (or
    strained natural yogurt)

5 ml (1 level tsp) good quality instant
    coffee granules
15 g ($\frac{1}{2}$ oz) molasses sugar

TO SERVE:
biscuits, chocolate sticks or wafers

Peel then thinly slice the bananas into the glass goblets or dishes in which the dessert will be served. Sprinkle with liqueur, lime shreds and juice, and sugar, turning the fruit gently until coated.

Whisk the cream, coffee and the second measure of sugar together until soft peaks form. Spoon over the fruit. Serve these desserts straight away or else refrigerate, to serve at a later time, chilled. (If using yogurt, fold the coffee and sugar throughout but do not attempt to whisk.)

Other soft, velvety-textured fruits could be substituted for the banana, (e.g. mango, persimmons, figs). It is the fruit, lime and creamy coffee combination which is such a unique blend of tastes.

Accompany with crisp biscuits, slender chocolate sticks or wafers.

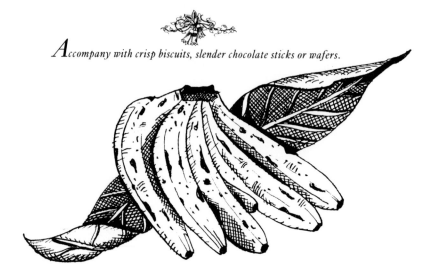

BERRIES IN THE SNOW

(Illustrated facing page 129)

A MOUTHWATERING FRUIT sculpture, this takes only moments to prepare yet its presentation is stunningly effective. The forms of the slashed open strawberries and the delicate husks of the cape gooseberries in their own syrup and under their dusting of icing sugar look medieval, beautiful, strange. This recipe merely underlines and emphasizes the sensuousness of two lovely fruits. As a dessert it is perfect in its understatement.

—— SERVES 2, 3 OR 4 ——

*40 g (1½ oz) or 8 physalis (cape
    gooseberries) complete with husks
175–225 g (6–8 oz) or 8 large red
    strawberries (with perfect, green hulls)
15 ml (1 level tbsp) fraise eau de vie
    de fruit (or other fruit brandy, or dark
    rum)
15 ml (1 level tbsp) icing sugar*

*TO SERVE:
iced fraise eau de vie (as above) in
    tiny chilled glasses*

Pull apart the physalis husks to form 5 'petals' then cross-cut each gold-orange berry almost through.

Wipe (but do not wash) the strawberries. Leave on the green hulls, and make diagonal slashes 5 or 6 times in each, from tip almost to base. Fan out each fruit, to form a pattern.

Arrange (preferably on a dark-coloured dish, plate or lacquer tray) and sprinkle over the liquor of choice.

Sieve icing sugar over the fruits, the plate and even the rim, so that it forms 'snow'. Eat using the fingers, lifting the fruit by its stem. Serve straight away or within 30–45 minutes (although it can survive for several hours) for an exquisite effect, with accompanying extra eau de vie.

This could be served after or with a traditional cheese course, or could be accompanied by a bowl of chilled fromage frais into which has been stirred freshly grated or shredded orange zest for a very light dessert.

153

Peruvian Chocolate and Avocado Mousse

I N THE pre-Incan remains of Chan Chan, Peru, evidence has been unearthed to suggest that the townsfolk enjoyed avocado, even before 900AD. Avocados possess many charms, not least of which are 8 essential vitamins and 5 useful minerals. I always feel that cheap overripe avocados should still be given another moment of glory. The texture and taste remain even if the colour is impaired. What more sensible thing to do than to combine them with chocolate syrup, home made? Season it as you like: the whole procedure takes about 5 minutes from go to whoa. I approve of such recipes—easy, elegant, delicious and in my view, examples of good husbandry.

——— SERVES 4 ———

2 overripe avocados (soft to the touch, but undamaged)
30 ml (2 level tbsp) cocoa powder (not drinking chocolate)
15 g ($\frac{1}{2}$ oz) butter
15 ml (1 level tbsp) scented honey
50 ml (2 fl oz) hot water
1.25–2.5 ml ($\frac{1}{4}$–$\frac{1}{2}$ level tsp) powdered cinnamon or mixed spice
15–30 ml (1–2 tbsp) brandy, armagnac or dark rum

TO SERVE:
25 g (1 oz) slivered almonds (dry-toasted until dark coloured)
4 or 8 small, decorative, edible flowers (optional)

Halve the avocados, remove the pit and scrape the very soft, mottled flesh out, (fingers do the task nicely—this is a good test of whether the flesh is really soft), into a bowl. Mash with a fork.

Measure the cocoa powder (on *no* account use substitutes) butter, honey and hot water into a small saucepan. Bring to the boil, stirring, and cook until thick, bubbling and syrup-like. Pour over the avocado. Blend using a fork until a uniform colour is obtained.

Taste, add spice and the liquor of your choice. Blend again then divide between 4 small china cups, pots, stemmed glass goblets or glass dessert dishes. Top with the slivered almond fragments. Serve immediately, just warm or leave to chill (in which time the flavour develops somewhat), with an edible flower as a garnish if wished.

PEACH SORBET BELLISSIMO

FRESH PEACHES and champagne—these always conjure up in my mind's eye sunlit orchards, King Louis XIV, Venice, and the cocktail named Bellini. What inimitable style they all possess! Like blossom in springtime, peaches and champagne seem blissful partners. In this recipe the crushed kernels from the stones are added and the peach skin is also retained yet the result is pure delicacy. Homemade fruit sorbets and ices are so superior to the usual bought equivalents that it is worth the small effort and occasional extravagance—even if that involves champagne. The fascinating part is that good champagne, once opened, still keeps its high quality bubbles for hours. So keep the balance of the bottle, chill it and if nervous, cover it, then 3 hours later, when the sorbet is perfectly ready, offer guests or family a convivial glass of champagne along with the fine dessert. It will not be easily forgotten!

——— SERVES 4 ———

700 g (1½ lb) white or yellow clingstone
* peaches*
150 g (5 oz) icing sugar
5–6 peach kernels, (from crushed peach
* stones) chopped*

150 ml (¼ pint) medium dry champagne
* or méthode champenoise wine (see*
* below)*

155

Slice the peach flesh from the stones, skin and all, into a medium non-metal saucepan. Add the icing sugar and gently heat until the sugar and fruit have reduced to an aromatic mush—about 4–5 minutes. (Do not allow it to overheat.) Extract the required kernels from 5 or 6 stones.

Process or blend the peaches and sugar syrup, with the peach kernels, to a smooth purée. Cool quickly over ice, stir in the champagne and pour into a shallow, freeze-proof plastic, lidded container.

Cover and fast-freeze for 2½–3 hours, stirring from the sides to the centre after 1½, 2 and 2½ hours. (If a sorbetière is available, follow the manufacturer's instructions.) Remove from the freezer. Stir (using a gentle rhythmic motion) for 1½–2 minutes or until the ice is very smooth-textured but not crumbly. This process will contribute to a desirable texture when scooped or mounded with a spoon.

Serve in iced glasses or dishes, accompanied by a sip or two of champagne, and a leaf or two, or a touch of seasonal blossom if any is still available.

In my view white peaches make the most delicate ice, and it is worth making this dessert if and when you ever locate them, for it is so delicate and old-fashioned a taste.

ICED SOUFFLE-BOMBE CHANOINE KIR

THIS SEMI-FROZEN dome looks utterly memorable if served in summer surrounded by sprays of fresh jewel-like red, white and black currants on the stem, some accompanying leaves, and a pile of crisp biscuits (perhaps *tuiles*, *langues de chat* or *gaufrettes*). But even in mid-winter, made using frozen and thawed berries, it is splendid, and packed with vitamin power as well as flavour. Do not be tempted to use substitutes: proper Crème de Cassis is an essential part of its charm. Canon Kir was a resistance hero and originator of the drink Kir. (By all accounts, from friends who loved and knew him, he would turn in his grave if anything less than proper Dijon Cassis and white Burgundy were used, though, being a resourceful fellow, he would not flinch at the inclusion of gin, I fondly hope.)

—— SERVES 6–8 ——

15 g ($\frac{1}{2}$ oz) or 1 sachet of gelatine
45 ml (3 tbsp) white burgundy
225 g (8 oz) fresh or frozen black currants
225 g (8 oz) fresh or frozen red currants
75 g (3 oz) caster sugar
60 ml (4 tbsp) Crème de Cassis
45 ml (3 tbsp) dry gin

2 size 2 eggs, at room temperature
150 ml ($\frac{1}{2}$ pint) double cream
150 ml ($\frac{1}{2}$ pint) fromage blanc battu

GARNISH:
Reserve some perfect fresh fruit and leaves
(including a few white currants, if
available) for garnish.

Sprinkle the gelatine over the wine in a heatproof bowl. Stir, then allow to swell and become firm. Dissolve over boiling water.

Crush the berries with 25 g (1 oz) of the sugar in a non-metal pan. Heat quickly until the juices run and the fruit is hot but do not overcook. Leave over gentle heat. Add the gelatine to the berry purée and stir well until dissolved. Put aside.

Put the mixture, with the Cassis, into the bowl of a food processor or blender and process to a smooth purée. Cool over ice. Stir in the gin.

Whisk the eggs and the remaining 75 g (3 oz) of sugar together, until thick, pale and mousse-like. Whip the cream until it forms soft peaks. Fold into the fromage blanc battu. Fold the almost-setting fruit mixture firmly but quickly into the egg mixture, then fold this quickly through the cream-cheese mixture.

Turn into a 1.1 litre (2 pint) bombe mould, ring mould, pyramidal flower pot or cone-shaped mould, or a charlotte tin. Cover and fast-freeze for 2$\frac{1}{2}$ hours or until the edges are frozen, yet the centre barely firm. To serve, hold the container in tepid or warm water for a few seconds, or wrap in a wrung-out hot cloth for a few seconds. Invert in one brisk movement on to a chilled serving plate or stemmed glass stand. Chill again briefly if necessary. Decorate with reserved fruit, leaves and biscuits and serve.

EMILIO'S HIPPOGRAS

'VENUS IN the Kitchen' or 'Love's Cookery Book' is a fascinating collection of recipes edited by Norman Douglas in the 50s. My mother-in-law kindly gave it to me. In my edition there is a crisply appreciative but ascerbic introduction by Grahame Greene, worth having for its own sake. The book is an assortment of common sense, scholarship, the wildly impractical and the madly poetic. It is implied (or shouted) that these are intended as love potions, aphrodisiacs, endearments. The book is dedicated to one Emilio, plainly a beloved, worthy of the aged editor's last loving duty. So here is his beverage, Hippogras, which I'm sure can still warm the heart of many friends. I have used fresh root ginger (perhaps preserved ginger in syrup could be substituted) but I feel powdered ginger would give a sad and dingy effect so do not use it.

SERVES 4–6

25 g (1 oz) fresh root ginger, bruised or preserved ginger (drained of syrup)
8 cloves
25 g (1 oz) cinnamon sticks, slightly crushed

1 or 2 vanilla pods, slashed along the length
900 g (2 lb) white sugar
1.1 litres (2 pints) red Burgundy

Stick the cloves into the root ginger. Put the ginger, cinnamon, vanilla pods and sugar into a large, glass or china jug, crock, jar or bowl.

Heat 300 ml ($\frac{1}{2}$ pint) of the wine to simmering and stir it slowly into the contents of the jug until well dissolved. Add the balance of the wine.

Leave, covered, to infuse for the time it takes to summon the beloved(s) of your choice, or else a group of amiable friends.

In the original recipe, 30 g ($1\frac{1}{4}$ oz) were given as the first 2 measures, no type of ginger was specified, nor method given. I hope neither Emilio nor Norman Douglas would disapprove of my interpretation.

157

INDEX